The Pledge

The Pledge

YOUR MASTER PLAN

FOR AN

ABUNDANT LIFE

MICHAEL MASTERSON

WILEY

John Wiley & Sons, Inc.

Published by John Wiley & Sons, Inc., Hoboken, New Jersey.
Published simultaneously in Canada.

For general information on our other products and services or for technical support, please contact our Customer Care Department within the United States at (800) 762-2974, outside the United States at (317) 572-3993 or fax (317) 572-4002.

Wiley also publishes its books in a variety of electronic formats. Some content that appears in print may not be available in electronic books. For more information about Wiley products, visit our web site at www.wiley.com.

Library of Congress Cataloging-in-Publication Data:

Masterson, Michael.
    The pledge : your master plan for an abundant life / by Michael Masterson.
        p.   cm.
    Includes index.
    ISBN 978-0-470-92240-8 (hardback); 978-0-470-94927-6 (ebk);
    978-0-470-94926-9 (ebk)
        1. Success.   2. Self-actualization (Psychology)   3. Success in business.
    4. Finance, Personal.   I. Title.
    BF637.S8M315   2011
    650.1—dc22

                                                                    2010034714

Printed in the United States of America

10 9 8 7 6 5 4 3

To Stephen Covey and Dale Carnegie, who helped me learn the art and science of prioritization, planning, organization, and getting things done.

CONTENTS

ACKNOWLEDGMENTS

I would like to thank the following people for their help with this book:

Kim Lansdale for her efforts in finalizing the text and putting it all together in a cohesive package.

Suzanne Richardson for her work in selecting and compiling the essays in this book.

Jason Holland for his quick and enthusiastic work in checking facts and tracking down supporting data.

Judith Strauss for her efforts to make my sentences clean and comprehensible.

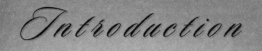

HOW TO LIVE YOUR ABUNDANT LIFE STARTING TODAY

We all want better lives, but too few of us are willing to make the changes necessary to have them.

Take my old friend Joe S., for example. Every time I see him—which is not very often these days—he complains about his (a) wife, (b) job, (c) kids, (d) body, and (e) friends. Usually he manages to complain about all those topics before he finishes a single beer. In the past I used to encourage him to change.

"Go to a marriage counselor," I suggested.

"They don't do anything," he assured me.

"Then get a divorce."

"It's cheaper to keep her."

All our early conversations went that way. Then I stopped making suggestions. Nowadays, when we meet, I have one beer and then get going.

Joe is an extreme example. He says he wants to change, but he doesn't really. He prefers to keep doing what he's always done. To lead a miserable life and waste his spare time complaining about it.

Joe is stuck. So is John K., a UK-based electrical engineer who had been reading my daily e-letter *Early to Rise (ETR)* for about three months when he wrote me. John said that although he regularly found "excellent" ideas in *ETR*, he couldn't get started. His problem: He "lacked motivation."

As an educated man, John could "recognize the opportunities present in . . . real estate, import/export, online, etc.," but couldn't get started on any of them unless he was "absolutely, 100 percent sure" that he would be successful.

He recognized that he was disabled by a fear of failing. But knowing you have an emotional problem doesn't mean you can solve it. "How can I get by this obstacle?" he wanted to know.

This is a book for people like John. People who want to improve their lives, but—for whatever reason—find they have been unable to do so.

HOW GOOD IS YOUR LIFE? TAKE THIS TEST AND FIND OUT

One of my favorite maxims is this: The quality of your working life can be determined by answering three very simple questions:

1. What will you do?
2. With whom?
3. Where?

I like the simplicity of that. And it makes sense. The amount of joy you have every day depends so much on making three wise selections:

1. The career you choose.
2. The business associates you choose.
3. The place you choose.

Chances are you've already made those three choices. You may have made them without much thought or made them passively by not choosing. But you are living with your choices.

Before we do another thing—and there are all sorts of wonderful things I'd like to do together in this book—let's review the decisions you've made.

Take the following three-part test. Then see what I have to say about your score.

What You Do . . . Your Career

Rate your business or career by assigning a number between 1 and 10 for each of the following questions. A 10 means it describes your business perfectly. A 1 means it doesn't apply at all to your business.

If you are an entrepreneur or professional, use this set of questions:

____ It is difficult to knock off because it has a unique selling proposition.

____ It is scalable: It can grow much bigger without my doing much more work.

____ It has a low overhead with low rents and no requirement for large capital investments.

____ It can be marketed well through the Internet and can take advantage of full direct marketing.

____ It has little or no inventory.

____ It is subject to few government regulations.

____ It is cash-flow positive. It can fund its growth through its own cash flow.

____ It has minimal labor requirements: It takes no more than four employees to generate $1 million in revenues.

____ It has an unlimited capacity to create wealth for me.

____ It challenges me fully—creatively, intellectually, emotionally.

If you are an employee, use this set of questions:

____ It takes advantage of my skills.

____ It challenges my logical brain fully.

____ It challenges my creative brain fully.

_____ It meshes well with my lifestyle.

_____ It surrounds me with interesting, intelligent people.

_____ It gives me the opportunity to excel and advance.

_____ It encourages independent thinking.

_____ It offers mentoring.

_____ It gives me a chance to learn new skills.

_____ It makes honesty and providing value to customers a top priority.

WITH WHOM YOU DO IT . . . YOUR PARTNERS, VENDORS, AND MAIN CLIENTS

Rate your business associates by assigning a number between 1 and 10 for each of the following questions. A 10 means it describes your business associates perfectly. A 1 means it doesn't apply at all to your business associates.

_____ Share my value system.

_____ Appreciate my strengths.

_____ Forgive my weaknesses.

_____ Make business deals beneficial to all parties.

_____ Share my ideas about what is right and wrong.

_____ Bring skills I don't have to the table.

_____ Are willing to talk through disagreements or misunderstandings.

_____ Do not exhibit bad behavior, such as verbal abuse of colleagues.

_____ Aren't prone to endless planning and preparation.

_____ Embrace new technology and techniques.

Now rate your key employees:

_____ Share my value system.

_____ Are productive and hardworking.

_____ Bring skills I don't have to the table.

_____ Support my business goals.

_____ Treat everyone, including competitors, with respect.

_____ Trust my judgment.

_____ Follow directions and advice.

_____ Are receptive to change.

_____ Do not panic at the first sign of defeat.

_____ Are always willing to learn . . . and teach.

WHERE YOU DO IT . . . THE PLACE YOU LIVE AND WORK

Rate the location where you live and work by assigning a number between 1 and 10 for each of the following questions. A 10 means it describes your location perfectly. A 1 means it doesn't apply at all to your location.

_____ Has my perfect climate.

_____ Has the physical qualities I love: mountains, seaside, etc.

_____ Has the population density I like: urban, suburban, rural.

_____ Has more than enough cultural/recreational activities for me.

_____ Allows me to enjoy a full life without a lot of traveling.

_____ Allows me to have a short commute to work.

_____ Has a comfortable, safe, and productive office environment.

_____ Has plenty of windows or an outdoor area.

_____ Has amenities such as gyms and restaurants close by for after work.

_____ Is well equipped, allowing me to do my job to the best of my abilities.

HOW TO SCORE

Each category has a total score of 100 (10 career questions times 10 points each; 10 business associate questions times 10 points each; and

10 location questions times 10 points each). Tabulate your scores and compare them to my notes:

- **90 to 100:** Congratulations! You have what you need. Improving your life in this category will be just a matter of tweaking the levers.
- **70 to 90:** You have accomplished a great deal. More than most people. But you can enjoy a better life in this category. Our master plan process will give you what you need to make the changes you want.
- **50 to 70:** Your life is better than most. (Most people rate their lives at between 40 and 50.) But you have a lot of room to improve. You need to master plan a new and better life.
- **Below 50:** You have made some bad choices. You may have to make some better ones.

Don't worry if your scores are lower than you hoped. Everything can be improved very quickly if you have the willingness to change. In this book, we'll talk about how you can have your best life possible.

OBSTACLES TO ACHIEVEMENT: WHY YOU CAN'T GET STARTED

John says he believes part of his problem is that he is not absolutely, 100 percent sure that if he starts working on some specific opportunity, he will be successful. How does he get past this obstacle?

Life takes on meaning when you become motivated, set goals, and charge after them in an unstoppable manner.

—*Les Brown*

The single biggest reason that people fail in life is that they *never take effective action.* Poverty is a problem, but not an insurmountable one. Countless successful men and women began their lives in poverty. Ignorance is a problem too, but that can be overcome by anyone willing to learn. Indecision and fear (of failure or success) are common obstacles to success. But all of these obstacles can be overcome, easily, by the individual who makes a commitment to take action, to figure out where he wants to go, and then to set one foot in front of the other in that direction.

Inaction is John's problem—not the fear that he will work on some opportunity that doesn't materialize!

Successful people don't sit around waiting for everything to be "100 percent" right or to be "absolutely sure" they will succeed. They assess the odds. And if the odds are reasonably good, they strike out boldly and energetically. They don't need absolute assurance, because they realize life doesn't provide any.

The cost of failure, successful people know from experience, is very modest compared to the cost of inaction. Failure means you are smarter the next time. Inaction means there is no next time. There is only a lifetime of unhappiness—first of worry and then of regret.

John is living in a world of worry now. If he doesn't take action soon, he will settle into a retirement of regret.

My rule is *Ready, Fire, Aim*. I have written about it many times in *ETR*, and it is the title of one of my books. As I explain in Chapter 17 of the book:

> *Ready, Fire, Aim* means disregarding most of the obstacles and detours that waylay others. It means finding and following the fastest path to any objective you set for yourself, so that time and all the problems time brings with it don't defeat you. *Ready, Fire, Aim* achieves more in less time, because it puts the correct value on *action*. It is also a realistic approach, because it acknowledges human imperfection and failure in an intelligent way. In effect, *Ready, Fire, Aim* is a way of increasing the success you have in just about anything.

Key to understanding the *Ready, Fire, Aim* approach is the principle of *accelerated failure*. The principle of accelerated failure rests on the recognition that we learn the most—in any enterprise—by making mistakes along the way. The faster we learn the critical mistakes, the sooner we acquire the knowledge we need to succeed. In other words, don't fear failure . . . seek it out!

John recognizes that *any* of the opportunities regularly discussed in *ETR*—real estate, information publishing, Internet marketing, and so forth—can be viable avenues for financial success . . . *no matter what the economy is doing.* That being the case, what is he waiting for? He's not going to increase his odds by waiting and worrying. The sooner he gets going, the faster he will make the mistakes he needs to make in order to succeed.

I am very sympathetic to John. You may be stuck in the same place. His problem is exacerbated by his intelligence. Smart people are good at worrying. They are adept at conjuring up reasons to fear failure and delay action. They are the victims of their own IQs.

John has to compensate for this by making a greater effort to ignore his worries and put himself into motion. It really doesn't matter which opportunity he chooses. He knows he is resourceful enough to succeed at whatever he does. All he has to do is get going. Put one foot in front of the other and start to move.

I am going to make that process easy—not just for John but for you, too, if you are in his shoes. I'm going to tell you what you need to do today. And then I'm going to tell you what you have to do if you want to become successful—and not just financially, but in every area of your life.

Ready? This is what you have to do today: Fill out the following pledge.

> *Okay, Michael. I am with you. I have committed to creating a master plan that I can use to succeed this year. I commit to following that plan without question or complaint. I further commit to keeping a journal on my progress and investing the time and money needed to achieve my goals. At the end of the year, I promise I will write to you and explain exactly what I have accomplished.*

I hereby pledge _____

*Name*_____

Date _____

That's it! Do it now!

I can't offer you an "absolute, 100 percent guarantee" . . . but if you are willing to take my advice and follow the master plan outlined in this book, I am willing to guarantee—99 percent—that this time next year you will be well on your way to health, wealth, wisdom, and happiness.

Is that good enough for you? If so, let's get started!

Part One

YOUR MASTER PLAN FOR AN ABUNDANT LIFE

WHAT DOES IT REALLY TAKE TO CHANGE YOUR LIFE?

I was 13 when I first heard the word "underachiever." Mrs. Growe, my ninth-grade English teacher, used it to describe a student who had, in her opinion, failed to work to his potential. The student? Yours truly.

"Mr. Masterson," she announced to the class, "is the classic example of an underachiever. He doesn't complete his work assignments. He shows up late for class and then wastes his time daydreaming. As a result, he produces C work. From a child with modest potential, I would be happy with mediocre results. In his case, I am very disappointed."

I was not surprised at the assessment. It was accurate. I couldn't deny it. The female maturation process held my interest at that time.

That and football. And goofing around with my friends. And just about anything else but schoolwork.

I wasn't a good reader. And I couldn't sit still during class. Much later I discovered that I was suffering from a combination of dyslexia and what is now called "attention deficit disorder." But neither Mrs. Growe nor I knew about such things then. As far as she was concerned, I was a perennial slacker. I shared her opinion.

The irony of commitment is that it's deeply liberating—in work, in play, in love.

—Anne Morriss

At least once a year, however, I promised myself that I would "turn over a new leaf." I sensed, as Mrs. Growe did, that I was not as dumb as my grades suggested. And I felt, deep down in my bones, that eventually I'd make a success of myself.

But before I could be successful, I had to change something very fundamental about myself. And that change began at the end of my senior year, when I woke up one day and realized I was disgusted with myself.

I was tired of being the perennial screw-up. I was sick of getting lousy grades and playing the fool in class. I wanted to become the person Mrs. Growe thought I should be. But it seemed to be too late. There was only a month to go before graduation, and it was obviously impossible to rectify four years of poor performance in so short a time.

Since my grades were mediocre, I had no chance of getting a college scholarship. And since my parents couldn't afford to help me with tuition, I had no choice but to attend a local community college. The community college was happy to take my $400 a year, and would be equally happy to give me the Cs I had been earning in high school. But I wasn't willing to live that life any longer.

I realized that, oddly enough, my lack of success was a benefit in disguise. I was about to put myself in an academic environment where mediocrity held sway—where I would be competing with other high-school screw-ups just like me.

What if I used the remaining time I had in high school to prepare for a new and better life in college? What if I directed my energy toward developing skills and habits that would help me succeed over the next four years?

And that's exactly what I did. The Saturday after I made my big decision to change, I drove my 1956 Bel Air to Nassau Community College in Hempstead, New York. I gathered together everything I could about the school and the curriculum I was going to be involved in. I brought it all back home with me and spent the rest of the weekend carefully reading every pamphlet and brochure.

I was doing something I had never done in school: getting ahead of my competition by planning my success. In the next few weeks, I became a minor expert in that little college. I knew every course they offered, every major they offered, and every teacher who'd be teaching freshmen that year.

Taking the initiative to plan my success gave me a very positive feeling. I could actually feel myself changing. I was becoming—even before I began—a serious and committed student.

I realized that I would be starting college as a brand-new person. None of my teachers would have heard about my high-school antics, and none of my fellow students would be expecting me to be the class clown.

Starting college without the bad reputation I had established in high school was like a gift from the academic gods. I could walk into my new classes as an interested, enthusiastic student who was there to succeed.

And that's what happened. I showed up for classes in September on time, prepared with the required texts. I sat in the front row and raised my hand whenever the teacher asked questions. I did my homework assignments and spent my spare time studying. Between attending classes, studying, and running a house-painting business on the side, I worked 16 hours a day, seven days a week.

By the end of the first semester, I had the reputation of being an A student. Throughout the rest of my college and graduate-school career, I never retrenched.

I sometimes think about what would have happened to me if I hadn't finally become disgusted with myself. Or if I had failed to make those preparations that allowed me to turn over a new leaf.

It's highly likely I would be grinding out a living somewhere, working a job I didn't like, struggling to pay my bills and making futile resolutions—knowing I'd live out my life as a habitual underachiever.

The difference for me was the simple realization that if I didn't change myself, my life wouldn't change—not then or ever. I had wasted my high school years making promises I never truly meant to keep. But I was tired of doing that.

Thinking back, I can see that there were several factors that allowed me to change in a serious and committed way:

1. I had bottomed out emotionally. I had finally reached a point where I truly detested myself for not achieving what I felt was my potential.
2. I made a decision to change completely—to go from being a C student to the top of my class.
3. I recognized that I would have to change not just my work habits but the way I thought about myself. I would have to "become" the A student I wanted to be.
4. And last, but not least, I took action immediately. I didn't wait till September to make the change. I started right away by *preparing myself to succeed* during my final months of high school.

Have you made resolutions that you've failed to keep? Held dreams of success and happiness that you've failed to fulfill? Do you sometimes feel that, however much you've done, you are still, in part, an underachiever?

If so, there is good news. Your past behavior has no bearing on your future work habits. If you can change the way you work—even just a little—you can change the way you live.

Most people reading this will think, "I don't need another motivational speech. What I need is a change of luck."

I'm here to say that luck had nothing to do with the change in my life. And it needn't have anything to do with whatever changes you would like to make in yours. Had I waited for luck to come to me, I might be waiting still. My life changed when I got fed up and started planning my success.

You, too, can change your life if you are:

- Dissatisfied with the lack of success you've had so far.
- Willing to make a big change—and not just a minor adjustment.

- Prepared to start working differently and thinking about yourself as a different kind of person.
- Willing to start now by preparing yourself to succeed.

REINVENT YOUR LIFE WITH A PROVEN PLAN FOR SUCCESS

Here's your challenge: a car race from New York City to Las Vegas. If you get there within a certain amount of time, you win millions of dollars and a completely new and better lifestyle.

Sounds like fun? Good.

Here's the problem: You don't know how to get there.

The countdown has already begun. In a few minutes, hundreds of other cars will be screeching away from the starting line. What should you do? Go out and buy a map? Have a navigation system installed in your car? Or start out at the gun with the rest of the pack and find your way by following them and asking questions?

Cautious people would install a navigation system and start the race late—drastically reducing their chances of winning. Successful people would use a combination of common sense and shrewdness: staying with the pack initially and then, by asking questions at gas stations along the way, making sure they were taking the fastest possible route.

Improving your life is a little like taking part in a cross-country auto race. If you wait too long to begin, you diminish your chances of finishing. Yet if you start off without any plan at all, there is a chance you'll get lost along the way.

When I decided to become an A student in college (after barely doing enough work to get Cs in high school), I started working on it right away. But I had a plan. And it was a plan that had been proven by countless A students ahead of me: Study the curriculum. Figure out which courses you have an aptitude for. Show up with an A-student attitude—and work your ass off.

That's what you should do if you are ready for success. Get started immediately. But use a proven strategy—something that has worked well for others.

INTRODUCING THE MASTER PLAN

Webster's New Collegiate Dictionary defines "master plan" as something that gives overall guidance for a project, such as the building of a church or school or city. Master plans are what real estate developers use to transform raw land into suburban subdivisions, urban centers, and waterfront business districts.

Washington, D.C., one of the most beautifully designed cities in North America, was once a swamp. Its transformation was the result of a master plan by Pierre Charles L'Enfant. And Columbia, Maryland, developed from rough farmland in the later part of the twentieth century, now accommodates a population of nearly 96,000.

I used a master plan to redesign a 3,000-acre residential resort on the Pacific Ocean in Nicaragua. Over 30 years of investing in real estate developments, I learned how helpful it can be to have a master plan in hand before you begin any major project.

> *People who cannot invent and reinvent themselves must be content with borrowed postures, secondhand ideas, fitting in instead of standing out.*
> —*Warren G. Bennis*

Master plans are also used to redesign companies. Jack Welch used one to articulate and execute his vision for General Electric. He said it was the key to transforming the corporate giant from a troubled, declining, billion-dollar company to a state-of-the-industry business leader.

And a master plan is what Warren Buffett and his partner used to turn Berkshire Hathaway into history's greatest financial success story . . . and themselves into billionaires.

On a personal level, my partners and I have used a master plan to help more than a dozen companies grow into multimillion-dollar enterprises, including one that went from $100,000 to $135 million in 11 years, and another that went from $8 million to $320 million in 14 years.

Master plans don't always work. The former Soviet Union and communist China were famous for their master plans, which continued to project growth as their economies gradually crumbled into dust.

For a master plan to be effective, it has to be realistic and flexible. It has to be realistic about resources and capabilities, and it has to be adjusted and/or radically changed when circumstances dictate.

But used properly, a master plan can achieve miracles. It can transform deserts into sparkling cities, debt-ridden companies into thriving businesses, and perennially underachieving people into healthy, wealthy, happy, and wise individuals.

How Is a Master Plan Different from a Plan?

A master-planned project differs from a normally planned project in its scope. Most large endeavors, whether they are real estate projects or business developments, are designed in pieces—one significant section at a time. That is not a bad way to create change, but it does entail wasted time, resources, and capital. Because conglomerating individual designs is always going to result in gaps, overlaps, and omissions.

When you master plan a project, you account for every aspect of it: the landscaping and water systems, as well as the architecture, electrical, and plumbing. By getting it all together at once, you can ensure an integrated finished product. You also reduce the time and money you spend fixing things that don't jibe.

The Dynamics of Your Personal Master Plan

A personal master plan can help you achieve all your life's goals quickly and with the least amount of trouble, time, and hassle. Using a master plan says you are serious about improving yourself, and that you want that improvement to be radical: from C to A. You will not be satisfied with B.

A personal master plan is a formal contract between the person you are today (fed up with the problems and lack of success you've been having) and the person you have decided to be (the successful you who is healthy, wealthy, happy, and wise). The personal master plan will help you reinvent your life, because it will force you to transform nebulous ambitions into specific objectives. It will spell out exactly what you have to learn, what you have to do, and whom you have to work with.

A personal master plan will change your dreams into tasks. In doing so, it may lose a bit of the romance. But it will compensate for that loss by giving you the exciting, uplifting feeling of progress. As each week goes by, you will be able to see, in very concrete ways, how you are improving. This will give your spirit a great lift and make it easier for you to continue making progress.

Most people never realize their dreams. Not because they aren't smart or shrewd or motivated enough, but because when they do make an effort, it is too little and misdirected. You won't have that problem. You have already begun your journey. And you will be using a map that has been proven.

Following a personal master plan is actually much simpler than randomly responding to a dozen separate impulses throughout your life. A master plan works because it reduces hundreds of minor and sometimes conflicting dreams and ambitions into four fundamental life goals. By simplifying your goals into four major ones, you will make it 400 times easier to pursue and achieve them.

I've changed my life three times. First, in 1968, when I went from being a C student in high school to an A student in college. Second, in 1984, when I decided to get rich. And third, in 2000, when I developed and began using a personal master plan for my daily e-letter, *Early to Rise*.

In every case, the changes were major, and the rewards were gratifying. But when I began master planning my success, the improvements came faster and easier. Were it not for the personal master plan that I developed during that time, I never would have been able to write and publish a dozen books. Or write, direct, and produce a feature-length film. Or write 350 poems in a year—all while keeping my "day job."

Using a personal master plan will put you on a new trajectory. It will take a few weeks to get everything in order, but soon after that you will start to notice the progress you are making. And before long (certainly within two months), you'll be amazed at how much you are accomplishing. Finally, you will be doing (and actually finishing!) projects that you have been dreaming about for years. As you knock off one objective after the next, you will feel your confidence growing, your skills strengthening, your wealth building, and your enjoyment of life increasing.

It is going to be a very good year for you: the year of your miraculous transformation!

Part Two

HOW TO TURN YOUR BIGGEST DREAMS INTO REALITY

ARE YOU SETTING GOALS . . . OR STILL DREAMING?

We all have dreams. We all carry movies in our minds about how life could be for us in a better world. Sally dreams of a big house with a built-in pool. Harry dreams of an eight-car garage filled with vintage Porsches. Jill fantasizes about painting pictures at the seashore. Jack wants that corner office with the view.

Chances are, Sally and Harry and Jill and Jack will never get what they dream about. They will go on playing those mental movies for themselves or talking about them to friends and family members.

Failing to live your dreams is not necessarily a bad thing. Lots of people are perfectly happy dreaming of one life but living another. The problem arises when the gap between fantasy and reality results in unhappiness or even depression. When this happens, it's time to master plan a new life. And the first step is to establish goals.

Goals are different from dreams in four ways. They are specific, actionable, time-oriented, and realistic.

1. **Specific:** Being rich is a dream. Developing a $4 million net worth is a goal.
2. **Actionable:** Winning the lottery is a dream. Winning a footrace is a goal.
3. **Time-Oriented:** Developing a $4 million net worth is a goal. But developing a $4 million net worth in five years is a better goal.
4. **Realistic:** Developing a $4 million net worth in five years is probably reasonable. Developing a $4 million net worth in four months is not.

Goals are also different than objectives—more long-term and broader in scope.

Your master plan will be broken down into seven-year and one-year goals, monthly and weekly objectives, and, finally, daily tasks that will make it possible to achieve your medium-term objectives and long-term goals. For example:

Seven-Year Goal: Develop a $4 million net worth in seven years.
First-Year Goal: Eliminate $36,000 worth of debt.
Monthly Objective: Land a part-time job netting $36,000 by year-end.
First Week's Objective: Get my first job interview.
First Day's Task: Write personal letters to CEOs of my top 10 "dream job" companies.

Okay, that's the plan. Starting today, you are going to be performing tasks every day that support weekly objectives that, in turn, support monthly objectives that, in turn, support yearly goals that, in turn, support seven-year goals. All of this will be done formally. All of it will be done in writing.

At this point, you may be wondering: "Does it really matter whether my goals are specific? Does it make any difference if I write them down?"

Glad you asked . . .

Why You Must WRITE DOWN Your Goals

It's very important to write down your goals. Carrying them around in your head is just not good enough. A study I discovered in *Look Within or Do Without*, by Tom Bay, explained why.

According to Bay, Harvard Business School did a study on the financial status of its students 10 years after graduation and found that:

- As many as 27 percent of them needed financial assistance.
- A whopping 60 percent of them were living paycheck to paycheck.
- A mere 10 percent of them were living comfortably.
- And only 3 percent of them were financially independent.

The study also looked at goal setting and found these interesting correlations:

- The 27 percent that needed financial assistance had absolutely no goal-setting processes in their lives.
- The 60 percent that were living paycheck to paycheck had basic survival goals (such as managing to live paycheck to paycheck).
- The 10 percent that were living comfortably had general goals. They thought they knew where they were going to be in the next five years.
- The 3 percent that were financially independent had written out their goals and the steps required to reach them.

These laudable results achieved by those who had become financially independent happened because they did more than set goals. They wrote them down.

Our life is composed greatly from dreams, from the unconscious, and they must be brought into connection with action. They must be woven together.

—Anais Nin

Here's some more evidence . . .

A recent study, from DayTimer.com, found that American workers with the highest incomes and most success in the workplace were those who had written goals. These superstars also had the habit of writing daily task lists stocked with prioritized steps to achieving those goals. On the flip side, of the more than 70 percent of workers who don't write down career or financial goals, only 9 percent of them accomplish what they set out to do each day.

It also turns out that there could be a psychological and even physical basis for the power of written goals. Here is what behavioral researchers Richard Molden and Steven Swavely had to say in a 2004 white paper, *The Psychology of Top Performers*:

> Writing down action plans provides a clear plan for getting there, and written time frames allow them to track their progress. This serves to increase the level of awareness for events, opportunities, and actions that can carry them closer to their intended goal.
>
> There is even evidence that written goals produce this elevated level of awareness through some very specific neuro-chemical effects on the brain.

And that's not the only research done in this area. Here's one study I read in *Psychology Today* (December, 1996) that shows the power of setting specific goals:

> Researchers from Virginia Polytechnic Institute and State University asked 56 female undergraduates to do as many sit-ups as they could in 90 seconds. One group, told to "do their best," averaged 43 sit-ups on each day of the four-day study. The other groups, which had been given the specific goal to do consecutively more sit-ups at each session, performed significantly better, averaging 56 sit-ups on the last day of the experiment.

Studies are great, but personal experience is better.

I spent the first 17 years of my life dreaming about success but having none. In my freshman year of college I decided to change that. I learned to learn and became an A student. Twenty-two years later, I discovered goal setting. Three years later, I was a millionaire. When I began writing *Early to Rise* in 1999, I learned how to prioritize my goals. That allowed me to achieve my first and most cherished dream: becoming a successful writer.

At *ETR*, needless to say, we set long-term business goals and medium-term objectives. This helped us grow our revenues from zero to $25 million in seven years. And it will help us grow to the next stage of our development, above $50 million, in the next few years. Using a master plan to grow our business is gratifying—but what's better is seeing our employees use personal master plans to improve their lives.

One, for example, used a master plan to go from being a low-level employee answering the phone to a management position in a few years. He is now a major profit producer for the company. Several employees have used master plans to meet their weight-loss and physical-fitness goals, including one who lost 30 pounds through diet and vigorous exercise and overcame significant health problems.

These laudable results happened because these people took the time to turn their dreams of wealth and health into specific, actionable, time-oriented, realistic goals.

You can spend your whole life dreaming. And dreams are wonderful things. By all means, dream away. But if you want to turn those dreams into reality, you need to transform them into goals.

What's your wildest, longest-held dream? How can you make it specific? How can you make it actionable? How can you put a time limit on it? How can you make it realistic? Use these four questions to create goals you can aim for . . . then take action. And you'll be living your dream in a few short years.

THE VOCABULARY OF ACCOMPLISHMENT

Words matter. They help us define meaning. We think with words. We learn with words. Words are the fundamental tools we use for communicating. If we use them well, we can cut and shape and polish our ideas precisely and beautifully. If we use them sloppily, we put ourselves at an intellectual disadvantage.

Words can help you think well. If you think well, you can plan well. If you plan well, you can work well. If you work well, you can accomplish almost anything.

Let's talk about accomplishment and the most common words associated with that concept: dream, goal, objective, job, and task.

To the sloppy thinker these words are all more or less the same. But to the individual who wants to achieve as much as possible in life, they are distinct—even worlds apart.

Here are some dictionary definitions:

- **Dream:** All of the primary synonyms that *Webster's* uses to define "dream" denote fantasy: nightmare, apparition, hallucination, illusion, and so forth. Antonyms listed: reality, verity, truth.
- **Goal:** Synonyms for "goal" include purpose, aim, and intent. Can you see the difference between dream and goal? Sometimes they are used synonymously, but they shouldn't be. A dream, by its very nature, is unrealistic—perhaps even delusional. A goal is not.
- **Objective:** According to *Webster's*, the word "objective" is identical to "goal." It has the same synonyms: aim, aspiration, and purpose. But I think there are two connotative differences between the two words. The first concerns time. Goals are longer in term than objectives. The second concerns scope. Goals are broader in scope than objectives.
- **Job:** A job is very different from a dream, goal, or objective. It is defined as a situation, post, place, position, appointment, operation, vocation, or career. "Job" describes the work you do for a living or at any particular time. It has little to do with goals and objectives. You can have a job without goals. You can have goals without a job.
- **Task:** A task is something smaller than a job. The difference is scope and duration of time. A task is some specific thing you are required to do, like mowing the lawn or editing a paragraph. It begins and ends within a defined space of time. Some tasks can be repeated. Even endlessly. But they are still very narrow in this regard. Sometimes "job" and "task" are used interchangeably. For our purposes today, let's keep them separated.

Okay. We have examined the terms for developing our master plan. How shall we use them?

In creating your master plan, we are going to talk about how to be very clear about establishing your goals. By distinguishing these five words, it will be easier for us to focus on what's important. Here's what I mean:

- **Dreams:** Master plans are not based on dreams, because dreams are, by definition, fantastic and delusional. Pursuing a dream may be a fine pastime for a fourth grader, but adults with responsibilities don't have time for dreams. They have to pursue challenging but realistic goals. So we are banning the word "dream" from our vocabulary. We are not wasting our time running after dreams. *We are pursuing goals.*
- **Goals:** As I explained in the previous chapter, goals are specific, actionable, time-oriented, and realistic. Being realistic doesn't mean they can't be lofty or even far-fetched, but they must be within the bounds of reason. You can decide that you want to win a million-dollar lottery within three years, but there is nothing reasonable you can do to win that million dollars except spend a million dollars on lottery tickets.
- **Objectives:** The dictionary I consulted didn't make a distinction between goals and objectives, but I'd like to make one that will help us talk our way through the master plan. Objectives, it seems to me, should be more specific than goals and also shorter in term.
- **Jobs:** Your job is what you are doing now. It has, as I've said, nothing to do with what you will be doing a year from now. And nothing whatsoever to do with what you will be doing in seven years. Putting a master plan into place means taking control of your future. Having a job means allowing someone else to be in charge of that. Therefore, for our purposes, it is not a good thing. We will put "job" in the same mental trash basket we tossed "dream" into. It is not useful to us. It is only a temporary necessity. It is something we will one day replace with "career."
- **Tasks:** Tasks are specific, time-oriented jobs that are part of a larger process. For the purpose of master planning your new life, we will distinguish tasks from goals and objectives. Tasks will be shorter in term and more specific than objectives.

When we are talking about your master plan, we will use these three words:

1. "Goals" for larger and longer-term desires.
2. "Objectives" for more specific, medium-term desires.
3. "Tasks" for very short-term actions that are required to achieve medium-term objectives.

I hope this doesn't sound like semantics to you. It is more than that. It is a little toolbox that contains three small tools that you can use to improve your life. Spend some time today thinking about how you currently work; how you set goals—if you set them; and how you pursue those goals on a yearly, monthly, weekly, and daily basis.

Have you spent your life chasing a dream? Pursuing some fantasy that never had any chance of being realized?

If you have solid, lifelong goals, have you converted them into something shorter and more attainable? Do you have multi-year goals? Or do you simply make New Year's resolutions? (I make resolutions. I do. But most of them are yearly objectives, based on longer-term goals.)

Do you write down your yearly goals? If not, I'll give you some data that will convince you that you should. If you do write down your yearly goals, do you also break them down into monthly and weekly objectives? If not, I'll show you why you should.

And finally: Do you spend at least 15 minutes a day planning exactly what tasks you need to accomplish? Do you establish priorities and time limits? Do you have a method for maintaining them?

If not, don't worry. We have everything you need to change your life and enjoy a brand-new lifestyle starting today.

BEFORE SETTING YOUR LONG-TERM GOALS, FIGURE OUT YOUR CORE VALUES

Before you can jump feet first into master planning your life, you have one more job to do: Figure out what's really important to you.

Most people you meet on the street don't like their jobs, are unhappy with their family life, and want more money. They believe that if they could just do this or that, everything would be better.

Winning the lottery would make it all okay. At least that's what they think. But the truth is otherwise. Unless you live your life according to your core values, no success will be enough to bring you joy.

So before you attempt to set your goals, you have to spend some time figuring out your core values. What do I mean by core values? I mean the feelings you have about good and evil that are buried deep within your heart.

What does goal setting have to do with core values? It's all about ensuring your long-term happiness. If you set goals that contradict your core values, you will wake up one day and say, "I did everything I said I wanted to do. But so what?"

You don't want to end up being yet another highly successful but fundamentally miserable person—a fate so common it's become a cliché. Here's how to make sure that doesn't happen . . .

Begin by imagining a funeral. It is taking place in an elegantly appointed room. The room is full of friends and family members who have assembled to talk about the deceased. You look around. You begin to recognize faces. "Who is the deceased?" you wonder. You look at the casket. Good God, it's you!

So what are the people at your funeral saying about you?

Imagine specific people: a parent, a sibling, a neighbor, a business associate, and even a stranger. Don't be vague about this. Think about individual, real people. And imagine them making very specific statements.

It's not enough to imagine your nephew saying something like, "She was a generous woman." You need to imagine a second, qualifying sentence, such as "She always sent me expensive birthday presents."

And be honest. Don't sugarcoat the pill. Say it like it is. For example, your next door neighbor might be saying, "I thought he was a very inconsiderate person. He never picked up the mess when his dog crapped on my lawn."

Happiness is that state of consciousness which proceeds from the achievement of one's values.

—Ayn Rand

Imagine everything the people at your funeral could truthfully say about you—and then think about the way their words make you feel.

If you don't feel good, it means that, in those relationships at least, you are not living your life according to your core values.

Now, for every negative statement you just imagined, ask yourself, "What would I like this person to be saying about me?" The answer to that question will reveal your core values for that particular relationship.

The goal of this exercise is to create a set of about a dozen sentences. Each sentence will be a statement that indicates what you think is important in a particular area of your life.

Let's say you imagined someone saying, "He was always struggling to make ends meet." That statement would make you feel bad, right? So then you imagine what you would *like* that person to say about you, and you might come up with, "He struggled for a while, and then everything changed. He became very successful and died a wealthy person." If that statement makes you feel good, it's reasonable to say that acquiring wealth is a core value for you. And you would write it down like this: "I believe that financial success is a valuable and admirable accomplishment."

Got it?

- **Negative Statement:** "He was always struggling to make ends meet."
- **Positive Statement:** "He struggled for a while, and then everything changed. He became very successful and died a wealthy person."
- **Core Value:** "I believe that financial success is a valuable and admirable accomplishment."

I recommend that you shoot for about a dozen statements, because you want to address all the major areas of your life:

- Your health values
- Your wealth values
- Your self-improvement (personal) values
- Your social happiness values

Why?

Because your core values should determine your goals. And your goals have to be comprehensive.

Most goal-setting programs are not comprehensive. They focus on just one thing. Making more money. Or losing weight. Or being happy (whatever that means). Setting such singular goals can sometimes be effective, if you have the flexibility in your schedule to focus on them.

But most people don't. And that creates a problem. They start out enthusiastically and make progress for a while. But before long, life's many urgencies push their way in. Good habits are neglected. Bad habits return. Before long, the goal is abandoned.

You are going to avoid that very common problem by considering the full spectrum of your life—not just your health or your wealth, but also your hobbies, personal relations, social obligations, and so on.

Here's what you should do now:

1. Take out a piece of paper and divide it into four boxes.
2. At the top of those boxes, write Health, Wealth, Self-Improvement, and Social Happiness.
3. Inside each box, write down statements in that category that you would like to have said about you at your funeral.

For example . . .

Health:
- "He was the fittest 80-year-old I ever saw."
- "He could run a mile in eight minutes."
- "I once saw him lift up a car by its bumper."

Wealth:
- "Of all the people who graduated from Riverdale High School in 1972, she turned out to be the wealthiest."
- "She had a huge mansion in Laguna Beach."
- "She left $4 million to charity when she died."

Self-Improvement:
- "He was the best chess player I ever knew."
- "He was also a published poet."
- "He knew more about home decorating than Martha Stewart."

Social Happiness:
- "She was the world's kindest mom."
- "She was also a very generous friend."
- "She was a strong supporter of breast cancer research."

Write down at least two such statements in each of the four categories. The purpose of writing them down is twofold: to fix them in your mind, and to have something specific you can refer to later.

You will be referring to these core values many times in the coming years. They should be a source of continuous inspiration. Treat them seriously. They are the crux of your master plan.

SETTING SEVEN-YEAR GOALS AND SHORTER-TERM OBJECTIVES

Now that you've learned how to come up with your core values— your basic beliefs about what is right and wrong in every major area of your life—you can convert them into long-term goals.

By long-term goals, I mean seven-year goals. Why seven years? Because it's long enough to get the job done, but not so far off that your goals seem untouchable.

I've written about this magic number in *Seven Years to Seven Figures* and also in *Automatic Wealth*.

Seven years is a common number when it comes to human enterprise. Economists often look at macroeconomic changes in seven-year cycles. The same period applies to business fluctuations, stock market movements, and even farming and natural cycles.

You can start and develop a multimillion-dollar business in seven years. You can master a language in less than seven years. You can become a black belt in almost any martial art in seven years. You can get healthy. You can get wealthy. You can get wise.

Seven years is as long as it has ever taken me to accomplish any of my goals: business or personal. And it's as long as I think it should take you.

So let's begin with seven years. After you have accomplished everything on your seven-year list, you can institute another master plan with yet another set of seven-year goals.

Establishing seven-year goals is easy. Start with your funeral statements. Convert them into a declaration of value. Then translate that value into a specific goal that you'd like to achieve in seven years.

For example:

- **Funeral Statement:** "He was one of the smartest people I've ever known."

- **Core Value:** Being smart is a valuable and admirable trait.
- **Seven-Year Goal:** To be accepted in Mensa by January 1, 2017.
- **Funeral Statement:** "She was the most generous person I've ever known."
- **Core Value:** Philanthropy is a valuable and admirable pastime.
- **Seven-Year Goal:** To give $1 million to the cancer fund by June 15, 2017.
- **Funeral Statement:** "He was the richest person in his high-school class."
- **Core Value:** Monetary wealth is a valuable and admirable achievement.
- **Seven-Year Goal:** To have a net worth of $3.5 million by April 21, 2017.

Do you see how easy this is to do?

Just remember the rules I mentioned earlier when determining your goals. Following these will greatly improve your chances for success.

First Rule: Your goal should be as specific as possible. *I will become rich* is too general. *I will develop a $4 million net worth* is specific.

Second Rule: Your goal must be actionable. *Winning the lottery* is a dream. *Winning a footrace* is a goal.

Third Rule: Your goal should be time-oriented. We have already talked about this and agreed to seven years. So make the goals you set today specific to seven years from now. *I will develop a $4 million net worth* is specific but not time-oriented. *I will develop a $4 million net worth by July 1, 2017*, is both specific and time-oriented.

Fourth Rule: Your goal should be realistic. Developing a *$4 million* net worth in seven years is probably realistic. Developing a *$4 billion* net worth is almost surely not.

So that's the first part of your assignment for today. Set a seven-year goal for each of your core values.

Your master plan will be based on these seven-year goals. But to turn those goals into reality, they must be translated into yearly, monthly, and weekly objectives. Here are the examples I mentioned earlier:

- **Seven-Year Goal:** Develop a $4 million net worth in seven years.
- **First-Year Goal:** Eliminate $36,000 worth of debt.

- **Monthly Objective:** Land a part-time job netting $36,000 by year end.
- **First Week's Objective:** Get my first job interview.

Do you see how that works? Each objective is based on the one that preceded it. It's really very simple.

So do that now. Set one-year goals for each of your seven-year goals. Write them down.

When you are done with that, create your first monthly objective. When that's done, create a weekly objective.

Do that today. That's plenty. Next, I'll show you how I create my daily task sheets. Tomorrow is the first day you'll be implementing your master plan.

USING DAILY TASK LISTS TO ACCOMPLISH YOUR GOALS

I didn't always plan my days. For most of my career, in fact, I didn't.

I had written goals. And I referred to them regularly. My goals kept me pointed in the right direction, but I was always moving back and forth. Often for no good reason.

Driving to work in the morning, I would think about my goals. That helped motivate me and often gave me specific ideas about what tasks I should accomplish that day. I'd walk into work meaning to complete those tasks . . . but by the end of the day, many of them were not done.

What happened? The same thing that may be happening to you right now. You sit down at your desk, and there is a pile of new mail in your inbox. You pick up the phone, and 15 messages are waiting for you. You open your computer and find that you've received 50 new e-mails since you last checked. You tell yourself that you will get to your important tasks later. Right now, you have to "clean up" all these little emergencies.

Before you know it, the day is over, and you haven't taken a single step toward achieving your important goals. You make an effort to do something, but you are tired. Tomorrow, you tell yourself, you will do better.

Does that sound familiar?

Productivity is never an accident. It is always the result of a commitment to excellence, intelligent planning, and focused effort.

—*Paul J. Meyer*

If so, don't feel bad. You are in good company. Most people deal with their work that way—even people who set goals and achieve them. Over the long term, they get everything done. But on a day-to-day basis, they are constantly frustrated.

You *can* be successful without planning your days . . . but you will have to work a lot longer and harder. The reason? When you don't plan your days, you end up working for other people—not just for yourself. You feel that before you get to your own work, you should first deal with their requests.

Starting your day by clearing out your inbox, voice mail inbox, and e-mail inbox is just plain dumb. Most of what is waiting for you every morning has nothing to do with your goals and aspirations. It is work that other people want you to do *for them*.

If you want to be the captain of your soul and the master of your future, you have to be in charge of your time. And the best way to be in charge of your time is to structure your day around a task list that you, and only you, create.

As I said, simply writing down my goals helped me accomplish a good deal. But my productivity quadrupled when I started managing my schedule with a daily task list. If you use the system I'm going to recommend, I'll bet you see the same improvement.

I have used many standard organizing systems over the years, but was never entirely satisfied with any of them. The system I use now is my own—based on the best of what I found elsewhere.

At the beginning of the year, I lay out my goals for the next 12 months. I ask myself, "What do I need to achieve in January, February, and so on, to keep myself on track?" Then, at the beginning of each month, I lay out my weekly objectives. Finally, every day, I create a very specific daily task list.

Here's how I do it . . .

My Personal Daily Task List

I begin each day the day before.

What I mean by that is that I create my daily task list at the end of the prior day. I create Tuesday's task list at the end of Monday's workday. I create Wednesday's at the end of Tuesday's workday.

I begin by reviewing the current day's list. I note which tasks I've done and which I have failed to do. My new list—the next day's task list—begins with those uncompleted tasks. I then look at my weekly objectives to see if there are any other tasks that I want to add. Then I look through my inbox and decide what to do with what's there. I may schedule some of those items for the following day. Most of them I schedule for later or trash or redirect to someone else.

In a spreadsheet, I create columns for the following:

- Tasks I will complete.
- Time I estimate it will take to do each one.
- Actual time it takes me to complete it.
- Tasks I will delegate to my assistant.

On most days, I end up with about twenty 15-minute to one-hour tasks.

I prefer to do this on my computer. You might like to do it by hand, in pen and ink. The point is to enjoy the process.

Because longer tasks tend to be fatiguing, I seldom schedule anything that will take more than an hour. If you have a task that will take several hours, break it up into pieces and do it over a few days. It will be easier to accomplish. Plus, you will probably do a better job, because you'll be doing it with more energy and with time to review and revise your work as you go.

A typical day for me includes two or three one-hour tasks, three or four half-hour tasks, and a dozen or so 15-minute tasks. The kind of work you do may be different, but I like that balance. It gives me flexibility. I can match my energy level throughout the day to my task list.

Ideally, you should get all of your important tasks and most of your less important tasks done almost every day. You want to accomplish a lot, so you can achieve your long-term goals as quickly as possible. But you also want to feel good about yourself at the end of the day.

You may find, as I did, that when you begin using this system, you will be overzealous—scheduling more tasks than you can possibly handle. So set realistic time estimates when you write down your tasks. And double-check them at the end of the day by filling in the actual time you spent on each one.

When you complete a task, scratch it off your list. One task done! On to the next one! I've been doing this for years, and I still get a little burst of pleasure every time.

Creating each daily task list should take you less than 15 minutes. The secret is to work from your weekly objectives—which are based on your monthly and yearly goals.

This system may not work for you, but I urge you to give it a try. I think you'll like it.

Before your colleagues, competitors, and coworkers are even sipping their first cup of coffee, you'll have figured out everything you need to do that day to make you healthier, wealthier, and wiser. You will know what to do, you will know what your priorities are, and you will already be thinking about some of them. You will not have to worry about forgetting something important. And you will have a strong sense of energy and excitement, confident that your day is going to be a productive one.

HOW TO MAKE MEASURABLE PROGRESS TOWARD YOUR MOST-NEGLECTED GOALS

As you've discovered so far, to master plan your new life, you must begin with long-term goals that correspond to your core values. From that good start, you must establish yearly goals and monthly objectives. Based on those, you create weekly objectives and daily task lists. Doing all that will help greatly. But if you want to really change your life, you have to learn how to prioritize.

Don't be a time manager; be a priority manager.

—*Denis Waitley*

I didn't always know how to prioritize. For much of my business career, I relied on goal setting and task lists and was happy with the results. But when I turned 50 and started writing for *Early to Rise*, I began to read how other business leaders achieved their goals. And that's when I discovered what a huge difference prioritizing can make.

The most important lesson I learned came from *The Seven Habits of Highly Effective People* by Stephen Covey. In that book, Covey presents a technique for prioritizing that impressed me greatly and soon became a central part of my planning process.

Divide your tasks, Covey says, into four categories:

1. Not important and not urgent.
2. Not important but urgent.
3. Important and urgent.
4. Important but not urgent.

In the "not important and not urgent" category, you would include things such as:

- Catching up on office gossip.
- Shopping online for personal items.
- Answering unimportant phone calls.
- Responding to unimportant e-mails.

In the "not important but urgent" category, you would include:

- Returning phone calls from pesky salespeople.
- Making last-minute preparations for an office party.
- Attending a required meeting that doesn't help your career.
- Planning for a meeting that doesn't matter.

In the "important and urgent" category, you might list:

- Making last-minute preparations for an important meeting with the boss.
- Making last-minute sales calls to key clients.
- Solving unexpected problems.

And, finally, in the "important but not urgent" category, you might include:

- Learning how to write better.
- Learning how to speak better.
- Learning how to think better.
- Working on your novel.
- Getting down to a healthy weight.

When you break up tasks into these four categories, it's easy to see that you should give no priority at all to "not important and not urgent" tasks. In fact, these tasks should *not* be done at all. They are a waste of time. Yet many people spend lots of time on them, because they tend to be easy to do and sometimes enjoyable in a mindless sort of way. Or they are afraid to get to work on important tasks, because they are afraid of failure.

Even worse than spending time on tasks that are not important and not urgent is spending time on those that are not important but urgent. They should have been dealt with long before they reached the crisis stage.

If you discover that you are spending a lot of time on unimportant tasks, you've got a serious problem. Unless you change your ways, you're unlikely to achieve any of your important goals.

So which tasks should you give priority to?

In *Seven Habits*, Covey says that most people think they should give priority to important and urgent tasks. But this is a mistake. "It's like the pounding surf," he says. "A huge problem comes and knocks you down and you're wiped out. You struggle back up only to face another one that knocks you down and slams you to the ground." You are "literally beat up by problems all day every day."

All urgent tasks—both unimportant and important—are problematic: They are urgent because you've neglected something or because they are important to other people (like your boss). In either case, you need to find a way to keep most of them from winding up on your daily to-do list. This means making some changes in your work habits—usually a combination of being more efficient and delegating more chores to other people.

Urgent tasks will burn you out. And turn you into an unhappy workaholic. If you want transformation in your life, you have to give priority to the important but not urgent tasks—because those are the ones that will help you achieve your major, long-term goals.

It's not easy.

The important but not urgent tasks whisper, while the urgent tasks shout. But there is a way to get that critical but quiet stuff done in four simple steps:

Step 1. When planning your day, divide your tasks into Covey's four categories: not important and not urgent, not important but urgent, important and urgent, and important but not urgent.

Step 2. You will, of course, have to do all the urgent tasks—at least until you get better at taking charge of your schedule. And you will have to find a way to get rid of the tasks that are not important and not urgent. But make sure you include one important but not urgent task that, when completed, will move you closer to one of your long-term goals.

Step 3. Highlight that important but not urgent task on your to-do list. Make it your number one priority for the day.

Step 4. Do that task first—before you do anything else.

Initially, you will find it difficult to do an important but not urgent task first. There are reasons for that.

- Since it is not urgent, you don't feel like it's important. But it is.
- Since it supports a goal you've been putting off, you are in the habit of neglecting it.
- You are in the habit of neglecting it because you don't think it's important and because you might be afraid of doing it.
- You might be afraid of doing it because you know, deep down inside, that it will change your life. And change, even good change, is scary.

But once you start using this little four-step technique, you'll notice something right away.

The first thing you'll notice is how good you feel. Accomplishing something you've been putting off is energizing. It will erase some doubts you have about yourself—doubts caused by years of "never getting to" your long-term goals.

That extra energy and confidence will grow, and will fuel you throughout the day. This will make it easier for you to accomplish other important but not urgent tasks.

As the days go by, you will realize that you are making measurable progress toward your neglected goals. In just a few weeks, you will be amazed at how much you've already done. And in 52 weeks—a short year from now—you will be a brand-new, much more productive person.

That year is going to pass by anyway. You are going to spend the time somehow. Why not do it by taking charge of your schedule? Why not spend that time on yourself—on what's really important to you?

TRACKING YOUR SUCCESS: WHY YOU SHOULD KEEP A DAILY JOURNAL

It may seem a self-centered pastime, but keeping a journal is actually an excellent goal-setting tool. It can help you figure out a direction for your life, and then guide you where you want to go.

A journal you use for that purpose—recording, revising, and recommitting yourself to your goals—becomes a log of your successes, observations, achievements, problem-solving skills, and best ideas that you can refer back to again and again. But you can also include less serious subjects.

In my earlier years, I kept journals sporadically, usually when traveling or involved in some interesting project. I kept a journal for two years when I lived in Africa teaching English and philosophy at the University of Chad. I kept a journal twice during summer vacations— once in the French countryside and another time in Rome.

But when I started writing for *Early to Rise*, I began keeping a journal every day. I have done so pretty much nonstop since then.

Before my thumbs became arthritic, I wrote my journals in a book with a fountain pen. Now I do it on my computer. I liked the feel of writing out my words. And I drew illustrations, indulging my artistic fantasies. I can't do that anymore, but I can import illustrations from the Internet.

I use my journal to get my day started. As a writer, I face the same blank page/screen every writer faces each morning. Rather than wait for the proverbial flash of inspiration, I begin by opening up yesterday's journal entry, reading it, and using it as a springboard for the writing I will do that day.

My first effort is a sort of obsessive-compulsive account of the hours that have passed since yesterday's journal entry: what I've eaten, what exercise I've done, what work I've done, and so on. This is not meant for anyone else to read. (I'd be embarrassed if anyone did read it.) It serves to rev up my idling mind and limber up my fingers. I spend five minutes doing this, which is usually enough.

Next, I edit something that I wrote the day before. Often, it's a poem or short story. But sometimes it's an essay for *ETR*. This requires a bit more mental acuity. After a half-hour of that, I can feel the creative engine kicking into third gear.

Then I start my real writing. Fiction or nonfiction, this is the most important part of my writing day.

My journal is also the place where I track my health information— my weight, my blood-sugar levels, my doctors' appointments and results—as well as the progress I've made on other goals in business and my personal life.

I used to keep my goals, objectives, and daily task lists separately on a notepad. This past year, I've begun to include my weekly objectives and daily tasks in my journal, and that has worked out very well.

My sister, who is an art director for theater and film, e-mails her family copies of her daily journal when she is on set. These are filled with photos and comments about her unusual life. I've never used my journal as a communication tool, but I can see from her example how it could be done.

To me, a journal should be like your house. It should be filled with interesting things that reflect the person you are. I hate houses that are designed by professional decorators. You walk through them and they all look the same. You know the people who own them, but you can find no evidence of their personalities.

Keeping a journal can help you change your life. As I said, it can help you do better work, achieve your goals, communicate with friends and family, and get your working day moving. And it's a terrific way to leave behind a record of who you were and what you were doing during your voyage through life.

If you are keeping a journal or thinking about starting one, here are three ways to make that journal work for you.

Three Powerful Ways to Benefit from Your Journal

1. **Keep track of your goals.** Every month, I consult my list of yearly goals and monthly objectives, and I create a list of weekly objectives. And as I've already mentioned, I consult my weekly objectives at the end of each day to create my daily task list for the next day. I keep both my yearly goals and monthly objectives on notepaper—a throwback to my hand-written days. But I input my weekly objectives and daily task lists directly into my journal that I keep on my computer.

   I highlight my priorities on my daily task list in yellow and try to accomplish them all early in the day. And as I complete each task, I change its color from red to black on screen (the equivalent of scratching it out). This is a technique I'd recommend to you. The point is to give yourself a little psychological reward for completing your work.

   At the end of each day, I note which tasks I've completed and which I've failed to complete. I also note how long it took me to complete each task. This helps me get better at estimating time commitments in the future.

   The goal-setting aspect of my journal has become the most productive part. It may not always be the most fun, but it's critical to the success of my long-term plans.

2. **Stay creative and keep your writing fresh.** Writing in your journal every morning gets and keeps your creative juices flowing. You can record ideas for new products or services . . . draft memos to your team or letters to colleagues . . . jot down outlines for books you want to write.

3. **Remember things you've learned, books you've read, and observations you've made.** We all have great thoughts now and then. And what do we do with those thoughts? Scribble them on scraps of paper and then lose them, right? Nowadays, whenever I get a good idea, I make note of it by entering it in my journal and putting "NTS" (note to self) in front of it,

highlighted in yellow. It is easy to spot these highlighted entries, so I can be sure they will be put on my goal list and not forgotten (like so many of my good ideas were before I kept a journal).

I also record interesting facts and figures from my reading. (I make it a point to locate at least one useful fact or idea in every newspaper or magazine or business book that I read.) And I use my journal to list recommendations that I read or hear: a new wine to try, a new book, a new CD from a favorite singer, a new restaurant, an exotic destination that I want to travel to.

It's amazing how much good stuff you can accumulate once you get into the habit of putting things that interest you into your journal and highlighting them for future use.

So those are three important benefits of keeping a journal—but there are many more. A journal can also be a place to:

- Record snippets of conversations that you can use later when writing your next (or first) novel or screenplay.
- List reasons why you deserve a big salary increase (or reasons why you shouldn't be let go during your company's upcoming layoffs).
- Identify all your assets and their locations, so your spouse or children can get to them in an emergency.
- Index your favorite recipes, quotations, images, and so forth.
- Record the good deeds you've done and the blessings you've received.

Keeping a journal takes about 5 to 30 minutes a day—well worth it when you consider the payoff: It will help you make better plans and accomplish more with your time.

And when you get much older, a journal can give you an unexpected bonus: hours and hours of fun, reminiscing about your rich, rewarding, productive life.

Part Three

YOUR ABUNDANT LIFE, DAY BY DAY

HOW TO BECOME AN EARLY RISER

When I walked into the London offices of my main consulting client at 7:25 A.M. that first day, I expected the place to be deserted. I was surprised to find the lights already on—and when I approached my temporary office, I saw that Ben, Nick, Gary, and Woody were already there working.

"Good morning!" I chimed, feeling that I had come upon new members of my secret fraternity. "You boys are here early!"

"Early bird catches the worm and all that," Nick said.

I went into my office with a smile on my face. These four early risers made up half the creative team. The fact that they were at work more than 90 minutes before 9:00 A.M. impressed me. Their good mood impressed me even more.

I would have inscribed on the curtains of your bed, and the walls of your chamber: "If you do not rise early, you can make progress in nothing."
— *William Pitt*

"I am going to be able to accomplish something here," I thought.

You've seen the studies: Early risers are happier, healthier, and more productive at work. They stay in better shape, earn more money, and report that they are more satisfied with their lives.

Lots of people I've talked to say they can rationally accept the argument that early rising is good. But they can't muster up the emotional or physical energy to actually do it.

They tell me they are "night" people. They have more energy at midnight, they say, than they do at 9:00 A.M. In fact, they say, they'd prefer to go to bed in the wee hours and wake up at noon if their jobs/spouses would allow it.

There is some scientific evidence to suggest they may be correct. Lots of research has been devoted to sleeping patterns in the past few years, and it's clear that for some people (about 15 percent, I've read), "late to bed and late to rise" really is more natural.

But just because it's a little harder for you to be an early riser doesn't mean you shouldn't try. The benefits are just too great and too numerous to ignore:

- You will get more work done.
- You will accomplish more important tasks.
- You will advance your career more quickly.
- You will be more respected at work.
- You will make more money.
- You will have more time to exercise.
- You will be healthier.
- You will be happier.

If you'd like to become an early riser but are having a difficult time convincing your body to cooperate, follow this 12-step program:

Early Riser Step 1: Stop blaming yourself. It may not be a lack of willpower that is making you want to sleep till noon. It is more likely a combination of your genes, blood sugars, hormones . . . and bad habits. But aside from your genes, these are all things you have some control over.

Early Riser Step 2: Take melatonin, not chemicals, at night. To get up early, you have to get to sleep early. If you have trouble falling asleep, try taking a melatonin supplement instead of a sleeping pill. My personal physician, Dr. Al Sears, calls this hormone— which is produced by the body in response to darkness—"nature's sleep regulator."

Early Riser Step 3: Sleep in the dark. The less light, the more melatonin your body naturally produces. So block out as much light as possible in your bedroom. Use blackout curtains or shades, and open them as soon as the alarm goes off.

Early Riser Step 4: Get plenty of fresh air. Fresh air is good for sleeping and for wakefulness. If you sleep with the windows closed, get outside and breathe in some fresh air first thing in the morning.

Early Riser Step 5: Don't eat before you sleep. Your last meal or snack should be about three hours before you go to sleep. You'll sleep sounder and feel much better in the morning.

Early Riser Step 6: Don't use the snooze button. According to the Sleep Disorders Center at Children's Hospital in Philadelphia, you will have a much easier time getting up when the alarm first rings, rather than waking up, falling asleep again, and then waking up a second time.

Early Riser Step 7: Put flowers in your bedroom. Researchers at Harvard reported that "non-morning people" said they were happier and more energetic if they woke in a room with fresh flowers.

Early Riser Step 8: Brighten up your walls. Some studies have indicated that vibrant colors help activate the energy cells, so paint your bedroom a bright, cheery color to wake up to.

Early Riser Step 9: Stretch. Five to 15 minutes of stretching in the sunlight will do wonders to get rid of any stiffness that may have settled in overnight. Yoga stretches are especially good.

Early Riser Step 10: Exercise. Supplement the stretching with exercise. After stretching, I alternate between calisthenics (Hindu push-ups, sit-ups, and so on) and a PACE routine—usually sprinting or stair climbing.

Early Riser Step 11: Start the day with a smile. Before you even wash your face, do a set of 25 smile repetitions. Just stand in front of the mirror and smile as brightly as you can . . . 25 times. The physical act of smiling produces endorphins that will give you energy and drive.

Early Riser Step 12: Wake up just one minute earlier every day. It wasn't until I hit my 30s that I came to understand the value of waking up early. I was bringing home the bacon, as they say, having mastered the art of making money. But rising at 8:30 every morning left me no time to accomplish other goals. So I started setting my alarm for one minute earlier every day.

Soon I was up at 8 A.M. . . . then 7:30 . . . then 6:30 . . . and, eventually, at one point in my career, 5:30. (These days, I wake up a little later—usually 6:00 or 6:30.)

Rising early has given me the time to write fiction, study Spanish, get in great physical shape, spend more time with my family, and more. Become an early riser yourself, and there's no telling what you can accomplish.

A LIFE-CHANGING EARLY-MORNING ROUTINE

When it comes to personal productivity, we all have the chance to have good days or bad days.

Good days are those that leave you feeling good, because you have accomplished your most important tasks. Bad days are those that leave you feeling bad, because you have failed to do anything to advance your most important goals.

If you want to have a better life, you must fill it with good days. The best way to do that is to organize your day according to your personal priorities—doing the most important things first.

It's easy to do. Yet most people don't. Eighty percent of the people I know—and I'm including all the intelligent and hardworking people I work with—do exactly the opposite. They organize their days around urgencies and emergencies. Taking care of last-minute issues that should have been dealt with earlier. Or doing tasks that help other people achieve their goals while ignoring their own.

Doing first things first. It is a very simple discipline. Yet its transformative power is immense. It can change your life—literally overnight.

It changed my life. Several times, in fact.

I've used this amazing technique to write a dozen books, produce a record, and script and direct a feature-length film. I used it again last year to write 350 poems—one a day, after I began on January 15. And I am using it this year to get that book of poems published and to write six other books (five business books under the Michael Masterson pen name, and a novel with my personal byline).

It is the single best technique I know for change. And it's the fastest and easiest way to turn your life around if you are not happy with the way it's been going so far.

Doing first things first. Is that what you do?

Here's what I do:

- I get up early—never after 6:30 A.M.
- I get to work early—never later than 7:30 A.M.
- I spend my first hour doing a task that advances my most important goal.
- If I'm going strong, I spend the next hour doing the same thing. If not, I switch to a task that advances my second-most-important goal.
- I spend my third hour on another priority.
- Only after four hours of doing important work do I allow myself to deal with less important work and other people's urgencies.

By the time most people start wandering into the office—between 8:30 and 9:00—I've done at least an hour and sometimes two hours of work that is helping me achieve my important goals. Goals that correspond to my core values. Goals that will immensely improve my life.

That's how to begin a very good day!

I do this five days a week. And on weekends, I find at least two more hours each day to devote to my top priority. In a year, this averages to about 600 hours. Six hundred hours may not sound like much, but it is.

Six hundred hours is fifteen 40-hour work weeks. That's almost four working months! Think about it.

Here's what you can accomplish in 600 hours:

- Learn to speak a foreign language with moderate proficiency.
- Become a reasonably skillful ballroom dancer, with a good command of the swing, the foxtrot, salsa, and the hustle.
- Achieve a blue belt in Brazilian jujitsu or a brown or black belt in one of many other martial arts.
- Develop a decent singing voice and feel comfortable singing at parties.
- Write five 60,000-word books on a subject you know.
- Write and edit two novels or 350 poems.
- Write, direct, film, and edit a 30-minute movie.
- Start a multimillion-dollar side business.

Do any of those things sound interesting to you?

None of this should astound you. It's all good common sense.

But it's one thing to recognize a good technique and quite another thing to learn to use it. Most people who read this will think to themselves, "I should do that. I should wake up early and spend time working on my dream." They'll think it, but they won't do it. They may get into the office earlier, but when they do, they'll probably turn on their computer and read their e-mail.

You can change you life if you allow yourself to experience the natural, unbeatable advantage of doing your most important work when your body is fresh and strong.

Get up early. Get to work early. Do your important but not urgent tasks first.

YOUR PERFECT DAY! HOW TO ALLOCATE YOUR HOURS FOR MAXIMUM PRODUCTIVITY

We all have the same number of hours each day to accomplish our goals. Nobody, rich or famous, has more than 24.

How we use those hours determines our success.

At this point, I would like to cover the two most commonly asked questions on how to allocate time for maximum productivity:

- How many hours, in total, should I work?
- What sort of activities should those hours be devoted to?

In particular, I am interested in the number of hours that should be devoted to planning and preparation versus taking action.

I have always resented any time I've had to spend to get ready to do a job. I want to get to it immediately. I don't want to sit around researching the task, assessing potential problems, and then figuring out the best way to approach it.

This is especially true when I am inspired. Driven by some vision of what could be, I feel maniacally compelled to realize that vision as fast as humanly possible. People who work with me are sometimes stressed by my eagerness to get going.

I believe this drive to action has been a big factor in my success as an entrepreneur. But, in my early career, my disdain for planning and preparation was a major waste of time—mine and that of those who worked for me.

I can't tell you how many construction projects and marketing plans I had to trash and start.

As time passed, I begrudgingly accepted the necessity of getting ready. I still have the urge to get going on any new project immediately, but I've trained myself to take some time to assess the situation and make plans.

The balance between planning, preparation, and action I found was expressed perfectly in the title of a book on entrepreneurship I published in 2008: *Ready, Fire, Aim.*

The idea, in a nutshell, is this:

- Action is the most important thing. Careers and projects are killed much more often by a reluctance to act than by acting too soon.
- Still, some planning and preparation is helpful.
- Get it roughly right as soon as you can, and then start. You can work out the kinks later.

Thus, *Ready, Fire, Aim.*

That is a good general guide for how to organize your time. But it doesn't tell you how much time you should spend getting ready.

Earlier this year, I asked more than a dozen successful business-people how much preparation and planning they did each day. I was also curious to know how many hours they worked.

Here are the results of my little survey:

Seventy-six percent said they work more than eight hours a day. The range was wide—4 to 12 hours. But the average was 9.3.

Most of them considered "planning" to be a vital part of their day. In fact, as a group, they spend an average of an hour doing just that. But all of them felt that "taking action" was the most important part.

For nearly all of them, the workday begins early—before 9 A.M. About half begin at or before 8 A.M.

Many begin working before they get to the office by reading e-mail or gathering information from newspapers or online publications.

Not many—only about 20 percent—take work home with them at night. But a majority put in at least a few hours on the weekend.

Many took pains to say they "make family a priority after work" and "spend time with the kids during dinner or at bedtime." I couldn't help but be suspicious of these responses. I didn't ask if they were neglecting their families, but they seemed to want to assure me they were not. Maybe there was a little guilt going on there.

I thought it would be interesting to compare the results of my survey with my own practices, as well as with the work habits of Ben Franklin (*Early to Rise*'s muse) and Donald Trump, America's most visible entrepreneur.

A typical day for me looks like this:

Part One: Early Morning

6:30   Wake up, smile, think positively. Get dressed. Sprint, walk, stretch, and meditate on the beach.
              The first thing I do in the morning is sprint and stretch and meditate. This is the most important thing I can do (besides eating well) to ensure a long and happy life.

7:00   Shower. Get dressed. Eat a high-protein breakfast while reading the newspaper.

7:30   In my home office, spend a few minutes writing in my journal. Read poetry, philosophy, and so on, looking for one good idea.

8:00   Write/edit poetry or fiction.

9:00   Write/edit nonfiction book.

10:00   Write an essay for *Early to Rise*.

I devote three to four hours entirely to writing—which is one of my four top priorities. About half my writing time is spent on creative writing and about half on business writing. This reflects a balance that corresponds to my current goals.

Part Two: Midday

11:00   Go to office and have a protein shake while reviewing the day's schedule.

11:15   Do one important business task.

11:45   Meet with my assistant and assign tasks to her.

12:00   Train in jujitsu at the studio next door. Shower and change.

Jujitsu is a hobby for me. It strengthens me, expands my mind, humbles me, and invigorates me.

1:00   Eat a healthy lunch.

1:30   Business (Action!), such as business meetings or phone interviews.

I don't take any meetings until after my midday workout. (I've trained everyone I work with not to expect to be able to interrupt me in the morning.) Beginning around 1:30, my day takes a dramatic change: from a schedule devoted to my primary objectives to one that is devoted to others' needs. Most of the meetings scheduled during the afternoon, for example, accommodate the wishes of others. They have time to see me each day, but it's only after I have taken care of my own top priorities.

4:00   Two 15-minute meetings.

4:30   Return phone calls.

I return phone calls in the late afternoon. It's not a top priority for me. It's as simple as that.

5:00   Finish all high-priority tasks. Write two *ETR* briefs and a blog entry.

If I have a spare half-hour during the afternoon, I devote it to an important but not urgent task . . . like writing things that don't have to be done by a specific deadline.

5:30   Review and respond to e-mails.
My penultimate task of the day is to review and return e-mails. I used to do it twice a day. Now I do it only once.

6:00   Finish all high-priority tasks and plan the next day. This is the last task of my workday.

Part Three: Late Afternoon

6:30   Exercise or relax.
Feeling good about accomplishing most of my priorities, I often reward myself with a second workout, followed by a protein shake. Or, I walk over to a cigar shop two blocks from my office, where I can do some additional writing while enjoying an espresso and a fine Nicaraguan cigar.

Part Four: Evening

7:30   Go home and enjoy a glass of wine and a crossword on the porch.

8:00   Dinner and conversation with my wife.

9:00   Mindless entertainment.

10:00 In bed reading.

11:30 Lights out.

Add it up and you have the following 24-hour breakdown:

- 7 hours of sleep.
- 4.0 hours of planning, preparation, and reading.
- 8.0 hours of action.
- 5 hours of socializing, relaxation, and recreation.

How does this compare with Ben Franklin's schedule?
Here's how he recorded it in his autobiography:

4:00   Wake up and wash, breakfast.

5:00   (He didn't say.)

8:00   Work.

12:00 Read while eating lunch.

2:00   Work.

6:00   Think about "What good have I done today?"
6:30   Relax and recreate.
9:00   Sleep.

Because Ben left three morning hours unaccounted for, it's difficult to estimate his time blocks precisely. But assuming those three hours were equally divided between leisure (he was devoted to it), reading, and work, his 24-hour breakdown would look like this:

- 7 hours of sleep.
- 3.5 hours of planning, preparation, and reading.
- 9 hours of action.
- 3.5 hours of relaxation and recreation.

That's remarkably close to my schedule. Being a fan of Ben, I'm happy about that.

What about Donald Trump?

He gets up early, too—usually at 5:30. He spends several hours reading newspapers. (He reads half a dozen at a time.) He arrives at the office at 8:30 and works till dinnertime—or, if he has no dinner plans, till about 10:00 p.m. He's usually in bed by 11:00 or 11:30.

His workday consists of non-stop meetings and phone calls. Being in the construction and development business, it's safe to assume that one-third of that time is spent on planning and preparation.

So, roughly speaking, his 24 hours would be broken down as follows:

- 6.5 hours of sleep.
- 5.5 hours of planning, preparation, and reading.
- 9.5 hours of action.
- 2.5 hours of relaxation and recreation.

Interesting, don't you think?

Do this right now. Take a look at yesterday's calendar and figure out how your workday compares.

Remember, these are typical hours for entrepreneurs. If you are a doctor or a dishwasher, you might have a very different schedule.

Nevertheless, my guess is that—despite what we wanted to believe when we bought and enjoyed Timothy Ferriss's book *The 4-Hour Workweek*—being successful in life requires three or four hours of getting ready every day and eight or nine hours of taking action.

To maximize your productivity, try it for a few weeks and see how it works for you. Because the way you begin your day has a major effect on how productive you will be in the afternoon and evening, follow these four easy rules:

1. Begin with a high-protein meal for long-term energy production without a mid-morning crash. For me, it's two eggs on a slice of high-fiber toast, several glasses of water, and a cup of coffee.

2. Do something physical to wake up your body. For me, it's a combination of walking or sprinting and 15 minutes of stretching (usually yoga).

3. Make your first task a meaningful one. By meaningful, I mean an important-but-not-urgent task, something that will move you along toward a long-term, life-changing goal. For me right now, that involves writing poetry or fiction. For you, it could be something related to making money or advancing your career.

4. Do something to stimulate your mind. I like to read poetry or philosophy. I know it sounds pretentious, but it works for me.

The point is to do what works best for you keeping in mind your ultimate goals.

THREE STEPS TO SUCCESS: THINKING, ACTING, AND BREAKING UP THE DAY

Ultimately, accomplishing your goals all boils down to how you spend your time. What you do and what you fail to do.

Setting goals is easy. Establishing priorities is pretty simple, too. The tough part is *following through*. Fortunately, there are a few easy steps you can take to coach yourself through the process.

1. **You must recognize that good intentions are not enough.** Writing up a list of yearly goals or New Year's resolutions might make you feel great. It may even make you feel like you are on your way. But you can't claim to be making any progress toward accomplishing anything until you start *acting* on your master plan.

2. **Don't spend too much time thinking about your future success.** Imagining what you want out of life—the big house, the luxury cars, the yacht—may give you pleasure. But despite what the think-and-be-rich gurus say, it won't make you successful. You must spend most of your time *taking action*, not daydreaming about all the toys you will have "some day."

   Most of the most accomplished people I know—and in that group I include some success coaches who preach the think-and-get-rich philosophy—don't waste their time thinking about success. What they think about is how to do a certain task or solve a specific problem. They know that wealth and success will come to them if they have a good plan and follow it.

3. **Break up your busy day.** Once you begin to implement your master plan, you will find that you will want to keep working for hours and hours at a time. Because you will be making progress toward your goals, you will be energized by the work itself. (If this has not been your experience with work before, be prepared to start enjoying your days a whole lot more!)

The extra surge of motivation will be very useful in getting a great deal of important work done. You'll be working more intensely, more intelligently, and just plain longer and harder than ever. But because you'll be working longer and harder, you'll need to force yourself to take little breaks—three- to five-minute breaks to reduce stress, recharge your batteries, and ensure that your body is not stuck in the same position too long.

It's not easy to take breaks once you are in a groove. In fact, you may be amazed at how difficult it can be. Most of the successful businesspeople I know think nothing of sitting at a computer or being on the telephone for four to six hours at a stretch. This is a testament to the motivational power of having a master plan, but it still puts a lot of pressure on your body and brain.

To make sure you take the breaks you need, I recommend a very simple device: an old-fashioned egg timer. Gene Schwartz, the legendary copywriter who was instrumental in the success of Boardroom Reports and Rodale Publishing, never sat down to work without setting an egg timer for 33 minutes. When the buzzer went off, he walked away from his computer and did something else for five minutes. He said the habit made him more productive. He said it was an important part of the process that made him a success.

When I'm writing, I set my timer according to the writing objective I've set for myself. Since I'm currently working on many writing projects at once, my daily goal is usually between 300 and 1,200 words. It takes me, on average, about 10 minutes to write 100 words. Therefore, I can knock off 300 words in a half-hour, 600 words in an hour, and a full, 1,200-word *ETR* article in two hours.

As you've seen from my typical daily routine, that's how I break up my time—in half-hour or hourly segments with an occasional two-hour sprint. Between segments, I usually stretch backward and forward over a Pilates barrel I keep outside my office. Sometimes I'll go outside and just breathe in the fresh air.

Because my afternoons consist of meetings and phone calls that have natural breaks, I don't need my egg timer.

But like Gene Schwartz, I have found my mini-breaks to be very refreshing.

Sometimes, if I had a short night of sleep and an intense midday workout, I get very tired in the middle of the afternoon. When I feel that way, I lie down and try to nap for 15 minutes. I will do that anywhere and under any circumstances. I'm not embarrassed by it. I think people who don't understand it should be embarrassed, not me.

Once, suffering from jet lag in London, I lay down on the floor underneath the conference table before a board meeting. Fifteen minutes before the meeting was to start, NR, a board member and multimillionaire German publisher, came in. Our eyes met. I thought he might say something. Instead, he took off his shoes, lay down next to me, and we both enjoyed a power nap.

I have outfitted both my home office and *ETR* headquarters with efficient workstations and comfortable chairs. And I have pillows handy in case I need a nap.

All these little breaks and naps and rewards enhance the pleasure of my day. No matter how much work I have on my task sheet, I'm never more than two hours away from some pleasurable experience.

If you find that your workday is one long trek down a dull road, try breaking it up the way I do and see if it doesn't make you happier and more productive.

HOW TO BE ON TOP OF EVERYTHING

As you put the master plan you're learning in this book into action, you will find that you will be able to accomplish more than you ever have before. Much more.

People will notice how much you're getting done. And, as a result, some of them will come to you for help. Or advice. Or simply to give you more work because you have become your company's go-to person.

This is all good and fine. It gives you more power. And more options. And more opportunities to advance in your career. But unless you have a system for managing all that extra work, you will soon be overwhelmed. And if you become overwhelmed, the happy movie you have been making about yourself in your head will turn into a horror story. People will be disappointed in you. Then angry at you. Before you know it, they'll be planning to get rid of you.

You don't want that. You want to be in charge of how much work you do. And you want to keep track of that work as well as all the work you delegate to other people. Keep in mind that the higher up you go in your business, the more delegating you'll be doing.

As you get busier, you want to get better, too. In particular, you want to:

- Be prepared for all the meetings you go to.
- Meet all your deadlines.
- Answer all the questions you've agreed to answer.

I am not, by nature, interested in details. I have always prided myself on being a "big picture" sort of person. I am pretty good at figuring out possible causes for problems and coming up with solutions.

And I can push to have them implemented. But I don't like keeping track of things.

I am also, by nature, a gregarious person. If someone asks me to do something, I like to comply. But I have found that my natural proclivity to please inclines me to take on more than I should. And that—in the past—often led to forgetfulness and missed deadlines, which led to disappointment and frustration.

Years ago, I realized that if I wanted to be able to run a company and lead smart, independent people, I would have to get better at keeping up with what they were doing. I could not afford the foolish luxury of excusing my insufficiencies in this area by crowning myself as a big-picture person. I had to adopt techniques and learn skills that would allow me to maintain control of the critical details of my business.

Since I had no natural inclination for organization, I was not able to conjure up any clever systems on my own. The organizational system that I started to follow then—and continue to follow now—is a composite of what I learned from several of my past mentors.

I've described my goal-setting, task-setting program in previous chapters of this book. It's based on establishing yearly goals, monthly and weekly objectives, and daily task lists, and then organizing those task lists in terms of priorities. The lion's share of my progress in personal productivity has come from using this program, and I can honestly say it has revolutionized my life.

What the program itself does not do is give me a way to keep track of the many details I need to be aware of in order to implement all those tasks effectively. Take a look at the section in Part Two on using daily task lists to accomplish your goals, and you'll see what I mean.

To keep track of the details, I use a very simple manual system consisting of two file folders. Here is how it works:

Documenting the Details

Let's say one of my goals for the year is to publish a book of some sort. To do what I personally have to do to get that done (write the book and approve the final layout and publicity), all I have to do is make the book a goal for the year . . . insert the appropriate monthly objectives . . . and then, based on that, put together my weekly and daily task lists.

But what about all the other work involved in getting the book published—the work I'm not going to do myself? What about finding someone to edit the book? What about the proofreading? What about getting a marketing team together and making sure they follow up with their plans? All of these necessary activities will be coordinated by my publisher. And since I won't be there during those discussions, I ask for a summary of the details to be sent to me by e-mail.

Filing the Details for Future Reference

When I receive that e-mailed summary, I usually skim it, just to remind myself of what it is about. Then I scribble some note at the top (such as "Ideas about publicity for new book"), and I file it in a folder I keep beside my desk. The folder has 12 pockets, one for each month of the year. I put the document in the appropriate one. If, for example, the first marketing meeting for the book will take place in April, I put the meeting notes in the pocket marked April.

When April arrives, I take those notes out of the folder (along with all the other documents stored in the April pocket) and insert them into another folder. This one has 31 pockets, one for each day of the month. I put the meeting notes where I think I'll need them. Maybe the day of the meeting. Or maybe a day or two beforehand, so I will have time to review them and prepare.

Out of the Folder and Into My Brain

As I've said, each night before I leave the office, I make up my task list for the following day. To do this I take out the following day's documents from the daily folder (the one with 31 pockets), and look at each item to reacquaint myself with the project it refers to.

Sometimes a quick review is all I need to bring myself up to speed. Sometimes I have to schedule some time the next day to study it. (Thirty minutes to an hour is usually more than enough.) Then, when it comes time for the meeting, I am equipped not only with the original notes in hand but with some fresh ideas stimulated by my preparation.

I use this system to keep track of just about everything. Projects I delegate to other people, projects I take on myself, and even correspondence I intend to answer later on. When I come across (or have sent to me) articles of interest, I often put them in the daily folder and bring them out to read one at a time.

It's a very simple system, but it has been a big help to me. And it allows me to see, very plainly, when I can't take on any new projects— because the monthly folder is overstuffed!

I am sure there are plenty of computerized programs that approximate what I do with these two folders, but those I've tried so far have proved to be cumbersome and time-consuming. I prefer to do it manually.

As the master plan I'm helping you build starts to change your life, you will begin to take on more responsibility than ever before. Don't count on your memory or natural intelligence to keep you on top of important details. Use this simple filing system.

FOUR THINGS YOU CAN DO TO GIVE YOURSELF MORE TIME TO BE MORE SUCCESSFUL

Of all the essays I've written about self-improvement, the ones that get the most response—both positive and negative—are those that have to do with saving time. I don't know why that is. You would think *Early to Rise* readers would be very happy to get advice about how to be more productive by spending less time doing routine tasks. You would think.

The biggest fracas was in February of 2005. That's when I suggested that *ETR* readers could save time by spending less time in the shower. I have friends, I told them, who spend a half-hour in the shower every day. That's crazy, I said. Two minutes is usually plenty for me. Five minutes tops.

Readers were outraged by this. They scolded me for my insensitivity. They accused me of being arrogant, sexist, and downright dirty.

Many people are apparently quite attached to their showers. For someone to even suggest they limit their time under the hot water puts them into a rage.

But that's not what this part of the book is about. It's about stealing time for yourself. So I am going to make a number of suggestions to help you find more time to invest in your future health, wealth, and happiness . . . if you are willing.

Limiting Your Shower to Two Minutes

I know how much you like to stand under the hot water and soak. I know how it relaxes you. But spending 15 to 30 minutes a day in the shower (as many people do) wastes a ton of water and time.

Save the planet. Improve yourself. Take shorter showers.

Amount of time you will save by taking short showers: 79 to 170 hours a year.

Eating at Your Desk

As I said before, I used to like hour-long business lunches. Then I got smart and started eating at my desk. I eat lunch at a restaurant two or three times a month. That's it. And it's always social. Never business.

Instead of letting vendors treat you to a fancy meal, let them spend their lunch money on giving you better prices.

Bottom line: Business lunches don't save time. They *waste* time! And money. Eat at your desk.

Amount of time you will save by eating at your desk: 250 hours a year.

Insisting on Very Short Meetings

I figure about 80 percent of all the hour-long business meetings I have ever attended need not have taken more than 15 minutes. Moreover, 50 percent of the multi-day business retreats I've been to could have been held in a day or a half-day.

Business meetings are like basketball games. Players spend most of the time throwing the ball back and forth while the score stays close. It's only in the last 10 minutes that they get serious and really play to win.

If you plan them well, you can significantly reduce the time you spend in meetings. Well-planned meetings have the following characteristics:

- They focus on a single topic.
- That topic is expressed concisely before the meeting in a short memo.
- The meeting is conducted by someone who encourages ideas but cuts off digressions and pushes toward solutions.
- The right people are there—never more than seven.

Time you will save with 15-minute meetings: 75 hours (assuming 100 meetings a year).

Answering E-Mails Efficiently

Answering e-mails only once a day—at the end of the day—saves me tons of hassles and passels of time. Why? Because three-quarters of the 100 e-mails I get every day are other people's concerns. It's much better for them, and more time-efficient for me, if I let them solve their own problems.

When I do answer e-mails, I make my answers short and to the point. When I have something difficult or negative to say, I don't use e-mail because it can cause confusion that results in many extra e-mails to clear up. Positive comments can be made very quickly. And if something can't be explained quickly, I do it in person or on the phone.

Every once in a while—maybe twice a year—I ignore my rule and start the day by doing e-mail. And I have noticed that when I do that, it takes a lot longer. That's because in the morning I feel like I have plenty of time and tend to write longer answers when shorter ones will do. I have actually tracked the time it takes me to do e-mail both ways. When I start in the morning, it takes about 90 minutes to get through 100 e-mails. When I wait till the end of the day, it takes between 45 and 60 minutes.

Time you will save by answering e-mails for only 45 minutes a day: 185 hours (assuming you check e-mail 250 days of the year).

The Impressive Total

Tally it up. I've just shown you how you can save 589 hours a year, at the very least. That is the equivalent of more than fourteen 40-hour workweeks!

Think of all the things you could accomplish with an extra 589 hours each year. Then make the changes and get going.

HOW TO CREATE A PERFECTLY ORGANIZED OFFICE

What does your office say about you? That you are orderly and businesslike? Messy but creative? Hopelessly overwhelmed?

Whatever your current habits are—sloppy or neat—you'll get more done and have less stress while you work if your office is intelligently organized. All kinds of studies have proven this to be so.

I've added at least an hour of productivity to my day by planning and organizing my work. A big part of that has to do with the physical organization of my office.

Here are 12 things you can do to make your office work harder for you.

1. Provide Yourself with a Range of Lighting, from Subtle to Very Bright

You will need three or four separate light sources. I recommend fluorescents (overhead or indirect) to light up the room brightly when you're feeling tired and need to wake yourself up. A second light source should focus on your desk. You can do that best with an overhead spot. A lamp, either on the desk or standing on the floor, will give your office a warm and friendly feeling when you entertain visitors. And natural light, shuttered with blinds, is great if you can get it.

If possible, have all your lights on rheostats (dimmers) so you can control the amount of light you need. And have them all switch on and off from the same place—preferably by the door.

The lighting in your environment may seem unimportant if you are not used to giving it any attention, but it has a direct effect on your energy and your mood. Use the best-quality lights you can afford.

2. Make the Space Workable

Your desk and credenza should be tailor-made to fit your working style. Don't shortchange yourself here. Give yourself sufficient room, but not so much that you will accumulate more stuff than you need. Make sure the files and equipment you use regularly are within easy reach. And position the furniture so that you can easily move from desk to credenza and back.

Put your computer on the credenza, not on your desk. That way, when people come in to meet with you, they won't feel like your attention is half on them and half on the computer.

3. Keep All Regular Reference and Inspirational Books Handy—Preferably within a Step and a Grab from Your Chair

This can be done inexpensively by furnishing your office with store-bought bookshelves.

4. Invest the Time and Money to Find and Purchase a Great Chair

From a personal productivity standpoint, your office chair is the most important thing you own. It is more important than your house—even more important than your car. Just think . . . on a typical day, you may spend 8 to 10 hours in that chair. Your chair is also one of the first things people notice when they step into the room. So make sure it looks good.

Adjust your chair so that your trunk meets your hips at 90 degrees, and tilt your computer so that the top line of the text is five degrees below your eye level. (That way, you don't have to move your head up and down to read.) Your keyboard should be positioned so that your hands lie flat. Set down a hard plastic mat on the floor beneath your chair so you can roll freely.

5. Keep an Egg Timer on Your Desk

I've already told you about this trick. Use the egg timer to make sure you are never seated for more than an hour at a time. Each time the timer rings, stand up before you turn it off. And once you are standing, get moving. Do something physical for five minutes. I stretch or do squats and push-ups. Sometimes I walk around the office and chat up my colleagues.

6. Get Rid of the Mess

You may think it works to your advantage to have everything you could possibly need piled up around you, but it doesn't. It just shows the rest of the world how unwilling you are to take control of your life.

"A place for everything, and everything in its place." That includes holders for pencils, pens, and reading glasses—separate and easily within reach.

7. Use Two Inboxes and Two Folders

The first inbox is the one that other people put stuff in. The second inbox is for you. Go through the first inbox every morning and select from it any important work you intend to do that day. Transfer that work to the second inbox. Take the rest of the stuff in the first inbox and file it in either your monthly or daily expandable file folders that I mentioned earlier.

Make sure the second inbox (*your* inbox) is cleaned out by the end of the day.

8. Have One or Two Drawers for Everything You Might Need in Case of an "Emergency"

In one of my drawers, I keep all the tools I might need at the office. Small screwdrivers (even a jeweler's screwdriver that fits the tiny screw that holds the arms to my reading glasses), WD-40, duct tape, and so forth.

In another drawer, I stash some backup clothing (two laundered shirts and two ties) so I can look good for an unanticipated but important meeting.

As it happens, I have my own bathroom at the office where I can stock a toothbrush and toothpaste, bandages, ibuprofen, hand sanitizer, cuticle cutters, and so on. But these items can easily go in one of your "emergency" drawers.

9. Hang a Clock on the Wall That Your Visitors Can See

Nod at the clock at the beginning of each meeting as you announce exactly how many minutes you have to solve the problem at hand. (Do *not* use the egg timer for this!)

10. Set Up an Old-Fashioned Bar

Stock it with scotch, vodka, and rum for those moments when kind words aren't enough. A humidor for cigars is optional for some, but not for me. If drinking is not your thing, try a Chinese tea service. I have a bar on one side of my office, a tea service on the other. They both come in handy.

11. Bring Some Life into Your Office

A live plant breathes back oxygen into the environment. It softens the hard surfaces, too. Select a big green plant, if you have room for it. Care for it on a few of your five-minute "egg timer" breaks.

12. Decorate Your Office with Signs of Who You Are as a Complete Person

Put up your family photos and your business awards. The walls and spaces of your office are gazing grounds for your visitors. Make sure the message they are getting is the one you want them to get.

And make sure there's at least one thing in your line of sight that makes you smile—maybe an inspirational quotation. Keep it there to work its magic until it loses power, and then find something new to replace it.

Invest in a sound system, too. You don't need anything fancy—just something that puts out soft background music.

One final thing that I won't put on the list because it may be too much to ask for until you are the boss: a daybed for a power nap when you really need one.

HOW TO CHANGE YOUR WORK HABITS AND BECOME A SUCCESS MACHINE

You are working on a blueprint for changing your life. You may be motivated to get to work on your plan but worried because you have never been able to work as hard as you know you will need to. You've made resolutions before. And you've even started to make improvements. But you have been distracted by problems and unexpected events. And you have stopped.

That's the big problem you face now. How can you make sure you keep on working?

The following story, which dates back 40 years, explains how I did it.

How I Became an "A" Student

Near the end of my senior year of high school, Mrs. Bigsley, the career counselor, called me into her office.

"I've been looking at your grades and your aptitude tests and your conduct reports," she said, thumbing through a stack of papers.

I waited expectantly. Mrs. Bigsley was the person in charge of getting students into good colleges and universities. "Maybe she's seen the potential I have," I thought. "Maybe she is going to help me get into an Ivy League school."

She put the stack of paper down on her desk and looked up at me.

"In all my years of teaching, I have never seen such a complete waste of DNA," she said. "Your parents are college teachers, are they not?"

I admitted they were.

"And your two elder siblings were 'A' students?"

"Yes, but . . . "

"And they went to top universities on scholarship?"

"Yes, but . . . "

"I've talked to Mrs. Growe, your homeroom teacher. And Mr. Dean and Dr. Mackel, too. They all say the same thing. You will never amount to anything that has anything to do with reading, writing, or math. Your grades support their opinion."

"But . . . "

"Your performance in high school indicates only one career choice as far as I can see: enlisting in the Army. I think you should talk to a recruiting officer. As soon as possible."

I tried once more to protest, but Mrs. Bigsley—and apparently my teachers—had come to a fixed decision. I was a complete and utter failure as a student.

It was *the* low point of my academic life. It was humiliating. I felt nearly defeated.

But Mrs. Bigsley's low assessment of me made me mad. I stewed about it that night and woke up the next morning with a completely new frame of mind.

I decided I would no longer be a screw-up. From that moment on, I was going to be a good student.

I started immediately by enrolling at the local community college. (If you had a beating heart, they accepted you.) Then I planned my summer. When I wasn't working, I would spend every waking hour reading and preparing for the classes I'd be taking.

Each day, I felt better about myself. I was learning what I should have learned in high school. Day by day, I was making progress.

Still, I was afraid that when I started classes I might revert to my bad habits. To make that scenario less likely, I found a "nerd" to share an apartment with and refused to sign up for any sports or pledge any fraternities. I also told my friends that I would be "out of touch" for at least a year. I explained my goals to them and asked them to respect me by leaving me alone until the following summer.

What I was doing, I realize now, was making a radical personality change. I was changing the way I thought about myself—not by thinking positive thoughts but by taking specific actions that made me *feel* like a good student.

When college began in September, I sat in the front row of every class, something I'd never done in high school.

I made it a point to always do at least 50 percent more than I was asked to do. If the assignment was to write a 500-word essay on religion, I'd write 750 words and include a glossary of impressive sources. If the assignment was to read *King Lear* by the following week, I'd read it twice. And then I'd go to the library and read critical essays about the play so I'd be aware of all the major interpretations.

I raised my hand *every time a question was asked*. And I turned in extra work, even when it would get me no extra credit.

In short, I turned myself into a full-blown hardworking, overachieving, "A-level" student . . . and I made sure my instructors, and my fellow students, saw me that way.

In the beginning, other students in my classes did as much work as I did. But as the weeks went by, many of them started slipping. Each time one of them fell behind, I was motivated to work even harder. And I was thrilled when I got those early test scores back. I had never before understood how good it could feel to get an A or B+.

Those good feelings motivated me to push even harder. With each passing week, the distance between me and the other "good" students widened. And by the time freshman year was over, I saw myself as a completely different person. I was no longer the funny screw-up I'd been in high school. I'd changed into the "Teacher's Pet" who sat in the front and had the right answer to every question.

Once my image of myself changed, my motivation became permanent. I was among the best two or three students in every class. I was going to keep that position, no matter how much work it took.

I maintained an "A" average for two years and easily got into City University—a tougher school—where I continued to perform well. Two years later, I graduated magna cum laude. Two years after that, I graduated at the top of my class at the University of Michigan. And later, at Catholic University, I received honors on my doctorate work.

Becoming top dog takes a lot of extra time, so you'll have to make significant sacrifices. You'll have to:

1. Get up early, and give your day a jump start by doing something meaningful . . . first thing.
2. Work late sometimes.
3. Do at least 50 percent more than what is asked of you.
4. Volunteer for challenging assignments.
5. Educate yourself on the side.
6. Become better than anyone else at the essential skills you need to accomplish your goal.

If you are like most people, your biggest distractions will be television, the Internet, friends, and family. Get rid of your TV. Limit your "recreational" use of the Internet to one hour a day. And let your friends and family members know that you won't be able to spend much time with them in the foreseeable future.

Work like mad until you've become number one in your class, job, or outside interest. When that happens—and it shouldn't take more than six months—you'll feel great about yourself. And once you experience that feeling, you'll never have to worry about motivation again.

Well . . . almost never. Everyone needs a motivational recharge once in a while. But after the first time, you'll understand exactly what you have to do to get yourself going again.

Part Four

CREATING A RICHER, MORE ENJOYABLE LIFE

MAKING OUR LIVES GOLDEN: THE CHOICES WE HAVE

Now that our last child is about to leave home, K and I are talking about getting television service. For about 20 years, we have been without TV. The idea was that our children would become better readers without the distraction—and that objective was achieved. All three of our boys are voracious and skillful readers.

So now, as empty nesters, we are thinking that it would be kind of fun to watch some shows together—to spend an hour after dinner, sitting next to one another, laughing at the same things.

To test this hypothesis, we jerry-rigged an antenna connection for the television combo set that we used to play only DVDs, and we spent a few evenings watching it.

The results of that experiment were mixed. There was something wonderful about watching those programs together—the double pleasure of the experience itself and knowing that your mate is "getting it," too. But when it was over, we found ourselves feeling like we used to when we watched television—which is to say a little sad and empty inside. As if we were mourning the time we'd lost.

The other night, we watched a science program together, a documentary about insects. Suddenly, we were having the experience we had hoped to have—sharing something that was both entertaining and illuminating.

That got me thinking about how people spend their recreational time—how much time they devote to it, the things they do, and whether the time they spend is spent wisely.

Broadly speaking, there are four kinds of activities we engage in: working, sleeping, eating, and relaxing. And it seems logical to assert that—up to a certain point of mental or physical exhaustion—the more hours you spend working, the more successful you'll be.

That said, we must acknowledge that all work and no play makes Jack a dull . . . or cranky . . . boy. We do need some recreation. The question is: How much?

And the answer to that is pretty simple. Just ask yourself how far you want to go in life. How smart you want to be. How high you want to rise in your industry. How much money you want to make. What accomplishments you want to achieve.

Determine how ambitious you are . . . and then find out how many hours of work were done per day by people who have already done what you want to do. Unless you are exceptionally gifted (or exceptionally slow), chances are you will have to work about as hard (i.e., as many hours) as they did.

Take the number of hours you sleep and eat and add to that the number of hours that successful people in your industry typically work. Subtract that from 24, and you will be left with the number of hours you can safely devote to recreation.

But there is another question that must be asked: Does it make any difference what kind of recreational activities you engage in? During your down time, does it matter whether you are sitting in front of the television watching Jerry Springer or lifting weights or playing a musical instrument?

Broadly speaking, there are three ways you can occupy yourself during downtime. You can amuse yourself with activities that, though fun, are harmful (like getting drunk). You can busy yourself with mindless distractions (like junky novels). Or you can choose to do something that requires a bit more energy on your part but will give you both a high degree of pleasure and the knowledge that you have somehow improved yourself (like practicing yoga).

It seems to me that whether it is the work we do, the sports we play, the vacations we take . . . we have the same three choices. We can do something that:

1. Improves us somehow.
2. Leaves us more or less the same.
3. Damages us in some way.

Look at almost any activity, and you will see what I'm talking about. In the books you read. In the friends you keep. In the jobs you take. You name it. Some choices will improve you and some will damage you . . . but most will fall somewhere in the neutral zone: They won't harm you . . . but they won't help you, either.

If we fill our lives with mediocre experiences—does that make sense?

Every day, we are given dozens of choices—from which foods to eat to which parts of the newspaper to read to which words to say in any given conversation. Many of those choices seem to be insignificant, but when you string them all together, they determine the quality of our lives.

At the lowest end of the scale, there's the person who spends his time using drugs, watching television, and prostituting himself or stealing to pay for his addiction. At the highest end of the scale—well, I don't really know who that is. But when I think of rich guys in limos or holy men on mountains . . . that just doesn't work.

Most of us live in the middle ground, mixing quality experiences with neutral ones while trying not to harm ourselves . . . but doing so anyway. We recognize that some of the choices we make are better than others, but we don't always have the willpower to make the better ones.

It's interesting, isn't it? The best choices are often the hardest to choose . . . because they require more of our energy. The worst choices are usually the easiest to refuse . . . because we are frightened by them. But when we have experienced them and found them pleasurable, they have the greatest pull on us. The neutral choices—the actions that do little more than get the job done—are the most popular because they are relatively easy and benign. They don't require much energy and they don't leave us hurting.

If there is one thing that life gives us all in equal portion, it is the hours of the day. We can't determine (with any certainty) how many hours will be allotted to us, but we can decide how to spend those that we have.

As I pointed out earlier, the more time you spend working, the more successful you're likely to be—but I acknowledged that even the most ambitious and hardest workers need to take at least a few hours out of the day to do something that gives them pleasure. Something that isn't work.

The question then becomes "What should that 'something' be?"

Think of the best choices—the ones that improve you—as Golden. Think of the neutral choices—the ones that just help you pass the time—as Vaporous. And think of the worst choices—the ones that hurt you—as Acidic.

It's up to you how much Gold, Vapor, and Acid you are going to have in your life.

When I think of my own choices—good, bad, and neutral—I notice that they have the following characteristics:

Golden Choices

My best experiences tend to be with activities that are intellectually challenging and emotionally engaging. Because they demand a lot from me, I shy away from them when I am low in energy. But when I do get into them, they build my energy and thus make it easier to continue. When I am through with such an activity, I feel good about myself and content with how I have spent my time

Vaporous Choices

These activities are easy to slip into and easier, too, to stay involved with. They are the choices we make when we don't feel like making choices. The time we spend when we don't much care how we spend our time. Welcome to the Vapor zone, the neutral, happy world of poker and sitcoms and gossip.

When I'm ready for some relaxation, my first impulse is always to choose a Vaporous activity. Having "worked hard all day," I want something simple and mindless so I can gear down. And most people would probably say the same thing. Getting into the Vapor zone is easy—and staying there is easier still.

The big problem with Vaporous activities—and this is a very big problem for me—is that they leave me feeling enervated instead of energized. And empty. Vaporous activities do for me what Vaporous foods (i.e., comfort foods) do: They fill me up but tire me out.

Acidic Choices

Everybody has vices. At one time or another, I've had just about all of them. I have never smoked crack, but I've done plenty of other things to destroy, reduce, or disable myself.

Why I do these things, I can only guess. Sometimes I think I need the challenge of surviving self-imposed obstacles. Whatever my reasons, the result of making those choices is generally the same. I get a dull pleasure that is mixed with a barely discernable level of pain. Even when the pleasure is intense, it is clouded by a foggy brain. It feels like I'm having a great time . . . but I am not sure. And if the actual experience of Acidic activities is mixed, the feeling afterward is not at all ambivalent. It is bad.

The interesting thing about Acidic options is how attractive they can be. Nobody would argue that they are good choices. We pick them because we are too weak to pick anything else, and we use what little mind we have left to rationalize our self-destruction.

Let's Take a Closer Look at These Three Categories

When we are at our best—confident and full of energy—we can easily choose Golden activities over all the rest. When we are feeling just okay, we can usually reject Acidic choices but find it hard to opt for Golden moments over Vaporous ones. And when we are at our worst—low in energy and full of doubt—that is when we are most susceptible to making Acidic choices.

Golden activities include:

- Meditation
- Yoga
- Watching an educational and inspiring documentary
- Listening to complex, uplifting music
- Appreciating art
- Watching a really, really good movie
- Reading a very good book
- Making love
- Tasting a really good wine

Vaporous activities include:

- Getting a massage
- Going to a sporting event
- Watching most "entertaining" TV like *The Office*, *CSI*, *The Tonight Show*, and so on
- Reading "beach" novels and page-turners
- Listening to most mood music, including most rock 'n' roll
- Having sex
- Drinking beer or whiskey

Acidic activities include:

- Getting drunk
- Listening to rap music
- Watching stupid/degrading TV shows like *Jerry Springer*, *Cops*, and *The Bachelor*
- Doing things you'd be ashamed to talk about

You may not agree with some of these designations. Not to worry. You can (and should) make up your own list. But in creating that list, consider the following:

When Choosing Gold . . .

The activity/experience is intellectually challenging. It teaches you something worth knowing or develops a skill worth having.

It is emotionally deepening. It helps you understand something you hadn't understood before and/or makes you sympathetic to experiences and/or situations you were closed to.

It is energizing. The experience itself charges you up spiritually, emotionally, and intellectually. You have greater strength and more endurance because of it.

It leaves you happy with your choice. During the experience and afterward, you have a strong sense that you are doing the right thing.

It builds confidence. Because you know that you are improving yourself, choosing Gold makes you feel better able to make wise choices in the future.

When Choosing Vapor . . .

The activity/experience is intellectually and emotionally easy. It feels comfortable and comfortably enjoyable. You have done it before and it amused you, so you are sure that if you do it again you will be equally amused.

It is usually passive rather than active. It is watching TV rather than going to a stage play. It is getting a massage rather than practicing yoga. It is chugging a brewsky rather than savoring a good wine.

It tends to be habit forming. Because it feels good (in a medium-energy sort of way) and is so easy to do, you find yourself doing it over and over again.

Doing too much of it is not good for you. Whether it's eating starch and fat or sitting on the couch and staring at the TV screen, a little bit doesn't hurt. But too much leaves you with the unpleasant feeling that you've wasted your time.

When Choosing Acid . . .

The activity/experience is physically or mentally damaging. Often, it kills brain cells. Sometimes, it gives you cancer.

Although it is bad for you, it is alluring. There is something about the way the experience takes you out of yourself that you find attractive.

It attracts bad company. Since most healthy people don't approve of it, you find yourself doing it with another set of friends. Eventually, you reject the friends and family members who don't "get it."

They are too straitlaced or lame to understand, so you figure you don't need them in your life.

It disables you intellectually, emotionally, and physically. During the moment, you are less capable of performing complex skills or dealing with complex emotional or intellectual issues. If you engage in Acidic activities a lot, you become less capable of peak performance generally.

Acidic experiences have ever-extending thresholds. What gets you off in the beginning is never enough to get you off later on. You have the mistaken notion that more is always better.

Will This Make a Change in the Choices You Make?

Once you've drawn up your own list of Golden, Vaporous, and Acidic activities, use it to keep track of the way you're choosing to spend your time. (A good way to do that is to make notes in your journal.) You may be surprised—and disappointed—by what you discover.

Make your own list. Track your own life. Ask yourself what you could become if—starting right now—you began making better choices.

In the meantime, I am going to have to talk to K about our plans for installing cable TV in our house. I will tell her my fears:

- That I will become addicted to it.
- That I will begin to watch the worst kind of shows.
- That in watching more and more Vaporous TV, I will spend less time on Golden activities.

She will point out that she is content watching her three or four favorite shows on video while she is on her Stairmaster. She will tell me, "Do what you want. It makes no difference to me"—and she will mean it. Which will make me entirely responsible for figuring out how much of my free time will be Golden or Vaporous or Acidic.

What about you?

REWARDING YOURSELF

When I was first getting into the business of selling educational programs, a famous zero-down real estate guru asked me, "Do you know the thing people who take my courses want most?"

I had a sneaking suspicion I was about to get it wrong, but I gamely answered, "To be successful real estate investors?"

He laughed. "You've got a lot to learn, my friend."

I took the bait. "So what do your customers want?"

"They want to avoid taking action."

I told him I wasn't sure I understood. He was kind enough to clarify. "Most of the people who take my courses and who will be buying your programs want to feel like they are on the road to success. But they don't want that road to end. They like the journey. They fear the destination."

"And why would that be?" I asked.

"To tell you the truth," he said, "I don't know. But I can tell you this. After our real estate students have gotten the knowledge they need to succeed, few of them get out there and get to work. Most of them just buy more programs. If they don't buy them from us, they will buy them from someone else. So we sell them extra programs."

"That's sort of depressing," I said.

"If you give one of my customers—someone who has completed his real estate education and is fully prepared to start investing profitably—a choice between actually getting to work and buying another course to learn more, he will buy the course."

"Are they afraid of failing?"

"Could be that," he said. "Could be they're afraid of success. As I said, I don't know."

Since then I've thought a lot about this failure-to-get-started problem. I've read dozens of books and talked to many of my colleagues and posed the question to hundreds of my customers. The theories as to why people don't take action are many and varied. The three that make the most sense to me are:

- **Lack of Confidence:** People who haven't yet been successful in life don't believe they can be, even if they are fully prepared to succeed.
- **Fear of Pain:** Some people see taking action as work and work as a form of pain. These are usually people who have never experienced the pleasure of working on something they value.
- **Laziness:** Besides the fear of work, human beings are programmed to be lazy. Being lazy means trying to get what you

want with the least amount of effort. Some people don't take action because they want to find an easier way.

If these are the main reasons why so many people don't take action when they are ready, what is the solution?

There's no mystery to that. Behavioral scientists know that the way to change a person's behavior is by motivating them through positive reinforcement. This is what B.F. Skinner had to say about it in *A Brief Survey of Operant Behavior*:

> It has long been known that behavior is affected by its consequences. We reward and punish people, for example, so that they will behave in different ways . . . . Operant reinforcement not only shapes the topography of behavior, it maintains it in strength long after an operant has been formed. Schedules of reinforcement are important in maintaining behavior. If a response has been reinforced for some time only once every five minutes, for example, the rat soon stops responding immediately after reinforcement but responds more and more rapidly as the time for the next reinforcement approaches. . . . Reinforcers may be positive or negative. A positive reinforcer reinforces when it is presented; a negative reinforcer reinforces when it is withdrawn. Negative reinforcement is not punishment. Reinforcers always strengthen behavior; that is what "reinforced" means.

Positive reinforcement is a big part of my life. I reward myself constantly and for almost any sort of accomplishment, big or small. By attaching rewards to my desired behavior, I increase the likelihood that I will repeat that behavior in the future.

When I "master planned" my life for the first time, I had to spend some time thinking about how to reward myself. I gave myself all sorts of incentives for all sorts of objectives. Some of them worked. Some of them didn't.

Some success coaches suggest big rewards for big accomplishments. You might, for example, reward yourself with a sports car when you make your first million dollars. Big goals like that never worked for me, because they were too far off in the future. What motivates me are short-term goals. And I have a feeling that short-term goals will be better for you, too.

Over the years, I developed a reward system that works very well for me. Here it is:

- As I mentioned earlier, when I complete a task on my daily task list, I cross it out (or change its color on my screen) to "signal" that I have accomplished it. This little gesture is like a tiny shot of adrenaline. It picks me up and gives me energy to attack my next objective.
- While working at the office, when my egg timer goes off, I get up from my chair, walk outside, and spend a minute or two stretching out my back. I've found that 30 to 60 minutes flies by—especially when I'm writing—and so these half-hour or hour-long periods seem very short.
- After I sprint in the morning, I reward myself with 10 to 15 minutes of yoga. Doing yoga might seem like more exercise to some, but to me it feels like a reward since it is so much more relaxing than sprinting.
- After training in jujitsu at noon, I treat myself to a tasty protein shake.
- At 6:30, I take my laptop to the cigar bar down the street, and work on my writing there for another hour or so. When I walk in, they have an espresso and water waiting for me. I look forward to this. I'm still doing work, but it's a reward because I'm doing it in a new place.
- After an hour of writing at the cigar bar, I reward myself by going home, breaking open a good bottle of wine, and having dinner with K.
- If I do any work in the evening, I reward myself afterward by reading a good book or watching a movie.
- I reward myself every evening by climbing into a great bed with silky sheets and a pillow that fits my head perfectly.

These rewards, as you can see, are pretty mundane. But that's the thing about rewards. They don't have to be big or even special. *They need only be enjoyable.*

It would be easy for me to consider these little things—the stretching, the protein shake, reading a good book—as simply an ordinary part of my ordinary day. But by looking at them differently, *by seeing them as pleasurable rewards for specific, desired behavior,* they motivate me.

I think that is the key—identifying little pleasures you already have in your life and using them as behavior-changing rewards. It's very easy to do once you recognize that these little pleasures are blessed gifts. Truly speaking, you are lucky to be able to enjoy them. Be happy about that. Use them pragmatically.

FIVE STRATEGIES FOR LIVING A SIMPLER, FULLER LIFE

About eight years ago, I did a little experiment. I wanted to find out if it really is possible to do business from anywhere in the world. So I packed my family off to Rome (one of my favorite cities) for a six-week "working vacation." I not only learned that, yes, it is possible for me to work in Rome (or just about anywhere else, for that matter), I also learned something that has had a much more profound effect.

In Rome, completely separated from the crazy, stressful routine I was used to back home, I learned how to simplify my life.

If you think simplifying your life will mean making less money, enjoying less success, maybe even being less effective as a business-person, think again. Simplifying your life is about having more—not less—of the good things. More passion. More meaningful work and relationships. And you can have more of those things by having fewer of the bad things—unsatisfying rituals, self-destructive habits, energy-draining feelings, and so on.

I'd like to talk about one way to simplify your life at work. If you follow my suggestions, you'll not only achieve more productivity but also gain more inner peace by avoiding emotionally costly conflicts.

We live in a time in which meaningless busyness keeps most people from achieving great things. They mistake being busy for being productive. They let the priorities of other people—their boss, their spouse, maybe even their children—take precedence. As a result, they feel swamped . . . and out of control.

You're not going to regain control over your life if you continue to try to deal with too many issues in too little time. As counterintuitive as it may sound, the only way to do it is to learn how to:

- Simplify that which is complex.
- Eliminate that which is superfluous.
- Know the difference between the two.

As an example, let's take a trap that I used to fall into all the time: getting involved in settling disputes between employees. Is it critical to your business that people get along? Yes. Especially since conflicts often get in the way of their working effectively. Is it up to you to drop what you're doing and help smooth the waters? No . . . not unless you want to join them in being unproductive.

So what should you do when the temptation arises to get involved?

Assure both individuals that they are bright and capable . . . or they wouldn't have been hired. Let them know that you have every confidence that they will find a way to settle the matter privately, between the two of them. And make sure they know that while it is uncomfortable for them not to be getting along, it is even less comfortable for the entire team.

Instead of spending hours trying to resolve a problem that has nothing to do with your own priorities, it will take only about 10 minutes of your time to build their confidence, show them that you support them, establish your expectation for a good-faith effort to resolve the conflict—and perhaps make both parties feel slightly embarrassed for making the rest of the group feel uneasy.

As long as you allow your quest for simplicity to be pushed aside—in favor of getting involved in situations where you don't belong, constantly checking your e-mail, going to pointless meetings, or writing long memos that no one reads—the ability to leverage your time and attention will continue to elude you. So will everything else that you'd like to accomplish in this lifetime.

Here's what you need in order to regain control—what I call the Simplicity Imperative:

Solid Vision: Whether you're managing a project, running a company, or handling your day-to-day schedule, you need a firm grasp of the big picture. Further, you need to be able to articulate your vision to others with clarity and ease and help them find ways to support it . . . not work against it. When we're not clear about our vision, we are at our most vulnerable. Our time and attention become diffused, and we start to lose focus.

Clear Priorities: Your priorities grow naturally out of your vision—out of knowing what's important and doing only that. Then, when you find yourself behind on reaching your goals, you don't have to look far to find the problem. Usually, it means you have lost control of your time because you stopped minding your priorities.

Daily Discipline: Perhaps the most valuable finite resource known to man is time. Squander it, and there's no way to get it back. Adhering to a daily schedule that is led by your vision and run by your priorities is the surest path to personal freedom. That might sound easy, but it's not. Most of us resist, and we pay the price. (It's not surprising that most serious diseases are stress-related.)

When compiling your daily to-do list, ask yourself these three questions:

1. "Is this something I could just as well delegate/eliminate?"
2. "Is there some way I could do this in half the time?"
3. "Is this related to an objective that will truly make my life better/richer/fuller?"

As I've said, in selecting my priorities each day, I highlight the most important tasks—the ones that are essential to my long-term personal master plan. And because I know I can do only a limited number of things each day, I start by doing those.

If I ever have to choose between two priorities, I ask myself: "Of the two, which one will be more important to me at the end of my life?"

It's all about economy—doing fewer things overall but making sure that the things you do have more importance.

Here's something else that can help you establish priorities.

Pareto's Law states that 20 percent of the things we do will achieve 80 percent of what we want. So ask yourself, "Which of the tasks that are before me are among that 20 percent?"

So, to simplify your life, you have to do more of what gives you soulful satisfaction and less of what gives you negative—or no—rewards.

Out with the bad. In with the good. In setting your goals and planning your time, keep that in mind.

Giving yourself the power to take control of your time really is the secret to success. And it will even make it possible for you to smell those roses along the way.

WANTING THINGS

I don't remember being thankful very often when I was a kid. I remember wanting things—lots of things—all the time.

I wanted toy trucks and cap guns and Lionel trains and baseball mitts. I wanted army men and model planes and erector sets. I wanted everything I saw advertised for boys on television. And everything other kids at school had, including boxed lunches and meat sandwiches instead of peanut butter and jelly in a paper bag.

I wanted to live in a nice house instead of the broken-down place my seven siblings and I grew up in. I wanted the new bikes and new clothes and professional haircuts my schoolmates had.

I wanted, as I said, all kinds of things. But gratitude? I didn't have much time for that.

Check that.

I *was* thankful to Bruce Conger's family for donating a box of his clothes to our family one Christmas. Bruce was the coolest dresser in seventh grade. I became, at least in my own mind, the coolest kid in seventh grade the following year when I wore his clothes to school. Tight, tight olive-green pants with creases so sharp they could cut you. Shiny black shoes with tips so pointed you could open a soda can with them. And sky-blue cashmere socks. Oh, was I cool!

I was also thankful two years later when my godmother, Jean Kerr, gave me one half of a share of one of her plays. It wasn't one of her big hits, but it was enough to buy me a brand-new pool cue that I used at the Rockville Centre Cue Club.

I was grateful, too, in my senior year, when, after having gotten caught in a riptide at Jones Beach and given up my life in an exhausting attempt to swim directly ashore, I was carried by the current around the jetty and back to safety. I had already lost my faith in religion at the time, but I was grateful. Very grateful.

Otherwise, as I said, I spent most of my emotional energy *wanting* things.

After high school, I was grateful that I wasn't drafted into the Vietnam War. Someone from my local draft board called me up and told me I was to report for duty, but they never followed up on that call, and I never heard from them again. I can only imagine that my file was lost. I still sometimes expect it to be found . . . and then find myself the oldest recruit in the Army.

In college, I developed an appreciation for learning and learned to be grateful for the great teachers I had. Harriett Zinnes, who taught me something about poetry, and Lillian Feder, who taught me to love good writing, were two of the best.

Then, after college and graduate school, I spent two years in the Peace Corps. I remember sitting on my porch in Africa, watching the rain pour down on my plaster-coated mud house and thinking, "You may get rich one day, but you'll never live in a house that will give you more pleasure than this."

I was grateful for that house—for having the privilege to live in it when so many of my students lived in shacks. And I was also grateful for my gratitude. I had begun to understand how good it feels.

When I returned to the States, a married man, I remember feeling grateful each time one of my sons was born. Grateful that they were all healthy. And I remember feeling grateful when, on Sundays, we would take the children on walks up and down 16th Street in Washington, D.C., to look at the stately mansions there. I was not envious of those elegant homes. Being able to see and appreciate them was enough.

In 1982, we moved to South Florida, and I took a job with a small newsletter publishing company there. I felt lucky to have the job—running the editorial department—because it meant that I was on my way to achieving my longtime goal of becoming a writer.

But two years later, I had a change of heart. I switched my goal from writing to making money. And when I did that, I stopped being grateful.

It was an interesting experience. I was fired up about making money. And I spent all my emotional energy pursuing it. But, looking back now, it's clear to me that I was once again preoccupied with *wanting* things. I wanted a higher income. I wanted money in the bank. I wanted a new car. And I wanted a mortgage-free home.

I've written a good deal about the tricks and techniques I used to acquire a lot of money during those years. But I never wrote about how ungrateful I was for the things that money bought me. I felt like I deserved them. And the moment I got something I wanted, I was thinking about the next thing I wanted.

When I turned 50, I realized that making wealth my number one goal had been a mistake. In doing so, I had learned a lot. But I had also lost a lot, not the least of which was my capacity for gratitude.

I am grateful now that I didn't lose my soul completely during those *wanting* years. And, yes, I realize that it's much easier to feel the way I now feel when you don't have to worry about expenses. Still, I feel grateful that I was able to make that change.

Lest you think I am grateful only for soulful things, I readily admit to being grateful for material things, too. I'm grateful for my 17-year-old NSX and my 8-year-old Ranger truck. I'm grateful for some of my clothes (those that make me feel good) and for my pool table (which I keep in my office) and to be living in a house that gives me as much pleasure as the mud house I lived in 30 years ago. (I was wrong when I thought that couldn't be possible.)

But when K and I talk about how grateful we are, the same three things always top the list:

1. We are grateful that we and our children are alive.
2. We are grateful that we and our children are healthy.
3. We are grateful to have so many good friends.

And I am personally grateful for being able to spend most of my working hours writing—which was my first and most important lifetime goal—and especially grateful that *Early to Rise* affords me 400,000 readers to write to!

What's on your list?

EMOTIONAL DETACHMENT AND THE ZEN OF GOLF

About a month ago, I played golf for the first time with Number Three Son (N3S). I was looking forward to a pleasant afternoon. I imagined fresh air, healthy sunshine, and that father-son banter that women who don't understand men categorize as superficial.

The afternoon started off as hoped for. The sun was shining. The course was green. We prepared by eating hot dogs and lighting up cigars. But on the very first tee, things started going badly. At least for N3S.

N3S is a novice golfer. He's played fewer than half a dozen games. He was focused on long drives and good chips and accurate putting. When he didn't hit the ball well—which was most of the time—he was angry with himself.

Though he may not have been hitting the ball the way he wanted, he was hitting it. I was impressed and told him so. "You are doing a lot better than I was at your stage of the game."

That didn't mollify him. By the ninth hole, he was emotionally exhausted. He didn't want to play anymore. "It's no use," he said morosely. "I stink."

N3S's frustration with his poor performance and his subsequent depression reminded me of myself until just a few years ago. It scared me to think that he might go through what I went through for 40 years. On the way home, I talked to him about one of the ways I've overcome my own tendency to get depressed. Today, I'm going to share that same strategy with you.

When you're happy, you can move mountains. When you're angry or depressed, your energy drops, your focus blurs, and your productivity lapses.

Depression can blunt your work skills. It can damage your reputation. It can separate you from your income and your possessions. It can affect your relationships with your spouse, your children and family—even lifelong friends. Depression will rob you of all the beautiful little moments that make life worth living—like a day on the golf course with Dad.

It steals your fun. It steals your time. It leaves you with nothing.

Two friends of mine fell into deep depressions when they lost their jobs and their income.

Both of them had based their self-worth on their ability to make money—a mistake that many entrepreneurs make. And when, through no fault of their own, they suffered a serious financial setback, they felt like failures. I suggested that the way to avoid falling into that trap is to base your self-worth on things that really matter—on personal values that have nothing to do with your income.

There's another common mistake that leads many to despair. The mistake that N3S was making during our golf game. I have to warn you that the solution to this one is a bit harder to understand and practice. But stick with me while I explain it. Because once you "get it," you'll have no trouble maintaining a positive outlook . . . even under the most difficult circumstances.

I am talking about developing the skill of *emotional detachment*. More specifically, developing the ability to set and pursue goals without caring whether you actually achieve them.

I learned how to do this only six or eight years ago, and have been practicing it in fits and starts. As each year passes, I get better at it. I feel happier and more in control of my life. Most important, I think it has helped me pass along some of my newfound happiness to others.

When most people hear the phrase *emotional detachment*, they think it means indifference or even heartlessness. Nothing could be further from the truth. Emotional detachment frees you from neurotic attachments and lets you focus your energies on other people, other things, and the here and now.

The best example I can give you is the natural love that a mother has for her child. When the child is happy, the mother is happy. When the child is unhappy, the mother instinctively wants to find the cause of the unhappiness and end it, if she can.

When the mother discovers that the child is unhappy because of some physical discomfort, she tries to relieve it. When the cause is an emotional conflict, she does her best to teach the child how to handle it. The mother's goal is always to prepare the child to become independent. She works consistently to gradually free the child from his natural dependence on her so that he can go out into the world and live a happy and productive life.

When an 11-year-old tells his mother that he "hates" her because she's imposed some restriction on him, the (mentally healthy) mother does not feel hurt, even though a hurtful thing has been said. She loves the child and doesn't take his statement to heart. She remains calm. She reminds him that she loves him. And she explains that the restriction will not be removed simply because he "hates" it or her.

In other words, she is *emotionally detached* from the child's expressions of anger.

If you are a parent, you understand what I mean. Most parents, most of the time, practice this sort of emotional detachment with their children. But there are some who can't do it, because they are emotionally attached to their children's approval of them. These are the parents who want to be "best friends" with their children. They break their own rules the moment their children object to them. Sometimes they go so far as to tolerate risky behavior.

The skill of emotional detachment can be applied to all relationships. It can work with your boss and colleagues at work. It can work with your spouse or parents at home. Detachment can also be applied to almost any challenge or problem. And the result will always be greater calmness and clarity.

This gets us back to my story about N3S. . . .

When I started golfing, I approached the game very much the way my son approached it. That is, I was concerned about the *outcome* of my shots. When hitting the ball off the tee, I cared about how far it would go. When I putted, I cared about how close the ball would get to the hole.

This made the game very frustrating. Being a beginner, the outcome of most of my shots was disappointing.

But it didn't take me long to realize that I was my own worst enemy. By allowing myself to be disappointed four shots out of five, I was setting myself up for failure. (How can you learn to play golf well if you are swearing when you are swinging the club?) The trick, I soon figured out, was to detach myself emotionally from the intended outcome (where the ball goes) and focus instead on the experience of the swing.

My goal, when I play golf these days, is to have a good swing. I don't care where the ball goes. All I care about is whether I achieve my *intention* of swinging the club properly.

This has made a remarkable difference in my game. In several short months, I have brought down my handicap by about 30 strokes. Before, I was shooting about 130 and hating the game. Now, I am hovering at 100 and liking it, even when the ball lands in a sand trap or rolls over the green.

Anything we do in life—any goal we set, any relationship we engage in—can be done better and more happily by applying emotional detachment.

Let me give you a few more examples.

Emotional Attachment: You want to go on a picnic Saturday afternoon. It rains. You are disappointed.

Emotional Detachment: You intend to have a picnic on Saturday. But, knowing you can never predict the weather, you consciously detach yourself from the hope that the sun will shine. You create Plan B—going to the movies instead. So when it rains, you move happily from Plan A to Plan B without getting upset or upsetting those with you. You are the Zen Master of your Saturday afternoon. You help others feel better by your good example. And that, in turn, increases your happiness.

Emotional Attachment: You want to get a raise. You don't get one. You are disappointed.

Emotional Detachment: You intend to get a raise. But, knowing you can't control the outcome of your next performance review, you come up with a Plan B that involves starting your own side business. You make a good presentation at the review, but your boss doesn't give you the raise. You aren't disappointed. In fact, you are excited . . . because now you can initiate Plan B.

Emotional Attachment: You want to marry your college sweetheart. You propose to her. She refuses you. You are crushed.

Emotional Detachment: You intend to marry your college sweetheart. But, recognizing that you cannot control her feelings, you detach yourself from that outcome and settle on Plan B, which is to enjoy the relationship for some months longer while you begin to look for a new one. You propose to her and are turned down. You aren't sad. You don't pout. You put Plan B into action. She notices your detachment and likes you better for it. Now it is up to you to continue the relationship or move on.

As I said earlier, the skill of emotional detachment is hard to understand and practice. But if you can master it, you will enjoy a life of unlimited wealth, health, and happiness.

Before N3S and I went golfing for the second time, I had him take a lesson with Larry, the pro I learned from. (Larry understands the Zen of golf. He, like Ben Hogan, understands that the true purpose of golf is not to achieve a specific score but to experience the serenity and pleasure that come with developing a consistently good swing.)

When we hit the golf course this time, I reminded N3S to focus his mind not on where the ball goes but on executing his swing. We played all 18 holes in perfect harmony. And though we didn't care about our scores, they were better than they had been the time before.

PUT A LITTLE LEVITY IN YOUR LIFE

I've recommended that you set goals to improve your health, grow your wealth, become a better person, and shake up your personal life. My recommendation for you today is a little different.

I want you to put a little Ho! Ho! Ho! into your life.

What, exactly, is Ho! Ho! Ho!? It's a technique that will:

- Reveal important truths to you about life and living well.
- Reduce tension and the troubles tension creates.
- Help you overcome obstacles, even seemingly insurmountable ones.
- Increase the dopamine in your system and make you feel better.
- Improve your blood circulation, respiration, and digestion.
- Greatly reduce the chance that you will die of cancer or heart disease.
- Make you a more popular person.
- Increase the speed at which you achieve your goals.
- Give you more personal power.

And the best things about this amazing technique are that:

- It won't cost you a dime to implement it.
- You don't need any special education or skills to take advantage of it.
- It takes only a few seconds of your time now and then.
- It gets easier to "practice" the more you do it.

Are you ready to learn more?

In 1992, during the height of the rioting in Los Angeles, Terry Braverman was driving along the Hollywood freeway during rush hour. Looking through the passenger window, he saw fires blazing in the city. The odor of smoke was mixing with the familiar scent of smog, and it was making the bumper-to-bumper drive seem somewhat dangerous. He glanced at his fellow commuters and could see in their faces that they, too, were feeling anxious.

Their anxiety made him feel even more anxious. He felt himself starting to panic. Then he remembered a simple maxim: You can't control what you can't control, but you are in charge of the way you react to it.

He decided at that moment, in the middle of the most nerve-shaking traffic jam he had ever been in, to lighten up. Luckily, Braverman had a way to do that. Being a professional comedian, he had a prop bag on the seat behind him. Reaching back, he pulled out a rubber clown nose. "This is just what I need," he thought.

Donning the clown nose, Braverman again looked out the window. At first, he said, the drivers around him were doing double-takes, as if to say, "He's a tourist. He doesn't know what is happening." But when he smiled, they got the message. "I wanted them to know that in spite of the circumstances, we can take a moment to lighten up and suspend the downward spiral of distress."

Reading this story in Terry Braverman's book, *When the Going Gets Tough, the Tough Lighten Up*, reminded me of that wonderful movie, *Life Is Beautiful*, about a father who heroically keeps up his son's spirits in a concentration camp by playing the clown. It reminded me also of Viktor Frankl's great book, *Man's Search for Meaning*, in which he tells about his own true-life experience of being in a concentration camp, and the amazing conclusion he came to after enduring the worst kind of human loss.

Frankl says, "As we see, a human being is not one in pursuit of happiness but rather in search of a reason to become happy. . . . Once an individual's search for meaning is successful, it not only renders him happy but also gives him the capability to cope with suffering."

In his book, Braverman also tells the story of Jean Houston, a philosopher and the author of *A Mythic Life*, who was traveling with a colleague to Washington, D.C., to speak at a conference that was meant to inspire attendees to be more creative. The colleague was complaining about how impossible it is to inspire creativity in government bureaucrats. "They spend their lives rearranging chairs on the *Titanic*. They are not going to listen to us," she said.

"We'll have to alter their consciousness," Houston replied.

"How?"

Houston explained that the best method she knew was through humor. So she was going to spend the first 10 minutes of her presentation making jokes. "At the peak of roaring laughter, one exists, as in mid-sneeze, everywhere and nowhere," she said, "and is thus available to be blessed, evoked, and deepened."

Houston's "method" is one that many professional speakers use. Audiences are often ill at ease in seminar situations. When you are feeling that way, you are more judgmental and resistant. But if a speaker is good enough to get you laughing, you will open up to him a little. You will feel, "Okay. I'm ready now. Tell me what you want and I'll listen."

Braverman tells how Rich Little saved himself from being beaten up by a bunch of thugs. "I was pretty scared, but within 15 minutes I had them laughing. I was doing my whole act. . . . So I turned that around I don't remember exactly how. I think I went into Louie Armstrong. . . . They didn't know who I was, but when I started doing the impressions they lost their incentive to beat me up." In this case, Little's humor did more than improve his own mental state—it improved his fate. At the end, he says, the thugs were applauding.

We've all been in situations where we allowed ourselves to be swept away by anger. Someone—misinformed or not—calls you a jerk or a jackass, and you respond with curse words and fury.

When I have used humor in difficult situations, it has never failed to help. At the very least, it made me feel better by putting things in context: Life is short. We live. We die. It's the same for all of us. Lighten up.

A great movie that touches on this subject was made in 1927. It is called *Sunrise*. It may take you 15 minutes or so to get into it, because it is in black and white and is silent, but invest the time. It is a powerful, moving story. And pay attention to the role that humor plays in it. It will make you want to be kinder and more loving. And it will show you how lightening up is so essential.

One of the most effective executives I know, the CEO of a major company, is a master of this powerful method of managing crisis. Because of his position, he often finds himself listening to senior managers who are upset about some real or imagined injustice done to them by some colleague in the business.

When I have been in similar situations—and I have been many times—my response was always to take the complaints of my managers seriously and try to work them out in a serious way. But "Chris" usually employs humor as his first response. He has a gift for making you understand how trivial your complaint is in the big scheme of things. I don't know how he does it, but he's done it with me a dozen times, and I can tell you it works.

Chris does a great job of resolving disputes because his first reaction to problems is to look for the Ho! Ho! Ho! in them. Most problems in life, it turns out, aren't as serious as they first seem. Those that are serious can still be dealt with better when you approach them with a lighter attitude.

So that's my wish for you—that you find time, when you are stressed, to find some lightness in your soul. It will give you the energy and flexibility to move forward with hope and happiness.

Part Five

THE PUSH YOU NEED TO SUCCEED

GIVE YOURSELF A KICK IN THE PANTS

I met Adela eight years ago, while she was attending her first American Writers & Artists Inc. (AWAI) copywriting bootcamp. (Like *ETR*'s info-marketing bootcamp, the copywriting bootcamp is now held every fall in Delray Beach, Florida.) She was an energetic, recently divorced, ambitious 36-year-old, bubbling with ideas. "This is the best conference I've ever been to," she told me at the end of the three-day program. "I can't wait to get back home and get to work."

I was excited for her. If there were ever someone who seemed charged up and ready to go, it was Adela.

When I saw her at AWAI's bootcamp the following year, I asked her how her freelance copywriting career had been progressing. "Well, I got derailed," she admitted. First, there was her father's death. That stopped her in her tracks. Then, she took a new job in another city.

By the time she had adjusted to that, she figured she'd be better off not trying to catch up. "I came to bootcamp this year ready to start again," she said proudly. "And I'm sure I'll succeed."

If attitude were all we needed to reach our goals, this woman was a future superstar. But attitude isn't enough. So I encouraged her to invest in *ETR*'s goal-setting program.

"I can understand how emotionally devastating it must have been to lose your dad," I said. "And I know how unsettling a new job and a new location can be. But if you make this goal—becoming a copywriter—your primary goal right now and follow our goal-setting program, nothing will distract you. You will be able to deal with any interruptions in your life." (I didn't think I had to mention that life is always full of interruptions.) "But while doing so, you'll keep making progress toward your primary goal."

She agreed to invest in the goal-setting program, and I didn't see her for two years. When I saw her at AWAI's bootcamp again and inquired about her progress, she was defensive. "I don't have the luxury of being able to spend six hours a day practicing my copywriting skills," she told me. "I've got a full-time job, a charity I work for, friends, family."

I didn't want to tell her that virtually everyone I've ever mentored has been in exactly the same position—or worse. And I didn't want to mention that when I was her age I held two full-time jobs and was married and had social obligations. What was the point in arguing with her anyway? She wasn't going to change. At least I was not going to be able to talk her into it. Somewhere in the back of her mind, she'd decided that what she wanted to do was just what she was doing:

- Continuing with a life that she herself described as "unfulfilling."
- Investing a week and a couple of thousand dollars every year or so to come to a copywriting boot camp and make herself feel better about her future.

"I just need to be inspired to get motivated again," she told me.

"Well, I hope this bootcamp can do that for you," I said.

I suppose it's okay to live your life this way. Who am I to tell this lady how to spend her time? Still, it makes me uncomfortable to see someone waste their opportunities.

Every year, because of the instruction and encouragement they receive at the AWAI copywriting bootcamps, dozens of people make the transition from employees to self-employed freelance writers. Many of them make the jump successfully after taking the basic copywriting program and even before finishing the Master's program. There is nothing the folks at AWAI like better than to receive that handwritten note or e-mail telling them, "Wow! I just got my first professional job!" or "Guess what? My latest direct-mail package became a control! I got paid $5,000 for a job that took me less than a week to finish!"

What makes the difference between those who succeed and those who don't?

Here's what I think: Successful "life changers" don't wait for everything to be "right." They don't wait for:

- Their personal lives to sort themselves out.
- Or their work to settle down.
- Or the projects they are working on to be completed.
- Or the new additions to their houses to be finished.
- Or the problems with their in-laws to be resolved.

Or . . . to be inspired.

Motivation follows action.

—*Robert Ringer*

Best-selling author Robert Ringer believes most successful people have this one trait in common: They don't wait for motivation. They create motivation through action.

"If I had to wait for motivation to write," he says, "I never could have written all the books I've written." (He's written about a half-dozen excellent personal-development books, including three bestsellers.)

"Like most writers, I spend many mornings staring at my computer, unmotivated and without any definite idea of what I'm going to write."

If he were in the habit of waiting for inspiration, he would spend too much time waiting, he says. What he does instead is "just start writing." It doesn't matter whether his initial writing is any good. So long as he keeps at it for an hour or two, he knows that something good will come along. "Motivation follows action," he says.

Unless you have a goal, make achieving that goal a priority, and find a way to act on it every day, your chances of succeeding are very slim.

With all my other business responsibilities—not to mention the writing I do for *Early to Rise*—I can come up with plenty of excuses every day to put off working on my next book. If I sat around waiting for inspiration to hit before I typed out a chapter, I'd never get anything done. Instead, I do what Robert Ringer does. I just start writing.

Frank McKinney, a multimillionaire real estate developer, has made the same point in a different way: "You don't need to wait until you are an expert to start making money in real estate. Get to know your local area by doing a little bit of work every day. Before you know it, you'll have a good idea about what to buy and when to sell, and then you'll be on your way to wealth and financial independence. But you have to start right away. Start immediately and then keep going. Do something every day, even if it's only something that takes five or ten minutes."

Whether you're an aspiring copywriter like Adela (who, as far as I know, is *still* waiting to be inspired to transition from bootcamp attendee to full-fledged copywriter), a would-be entrepreneur, or a mountain climber dying to tackle Mount Everest, get out there and do something—every day—to advance your goal.

THE JUNKIE'S SECRET

As a teenager I had the impulses of a junkyard dog. If someone looked at me "wrong," I started barking. This resulted in many scraps—most of them against bigger and more skillful fighters. I managed to "win" a great many of them, however, because I was able to tap into something inside me—some form of fury, I suppose—that fueled my aggression.

Something like that exists in the realm of wealth building. There is something that burns—or at least glows—inside you that can—if you tap into it—transform you into a money making megalomaniac (MMM).

And as an MMM, you will never:

- Have another sluggish moment.
- Feel confused about what you need to do.

- Doubt your ability to make money.
- Hesitate to go after it.

Does that sound good? Or scary?

If it sounds scary, don't feel bad. Most people are afraid of change—and most especially of *internal* change. What I am about to talk about is very much internal change. It goes deep. It stays long. And it changes the way you think and feel.

When offered a chance to change, most people think, "I'm not entirely satisfied with myself now, but I don't hate myself, either. If I change in some way I don't expect, I might lose control or become even unhappier than I am now. Better to stay the way I am."

But if it sounds good, you're in luck. I am going to give you the secret I used to fuel my money-making ambitions in the past and use now to motivate me to write books and make movies.

I call it *the Junkie's Secret.*

Consider the Humble Coke Addict

Take an ambitionless, aimless young man in his 20s. He's a high-school dropout, which means he's functionally illiterate. Having been deprived of a good family, he is also angry and unmotivated. To make matters worse, he is not the naturally bright but deprived young man you see in the movies. He's dumb as a dish rag.

Let me ask you: What is this young man likely to do for a living?

You guessed right—nothing.

But if he *were* to work . . . if he could be somehow forced to work through some amazingly successful government program . . . how much money could he make?

You guessed right again—about $48 a day or $6 an hour—before taxes.

Now take that same stupid, lazy kid and give him a good, old-fashioned, crack-cocaine addiction.

How much money could he make then?

You guessed it again—he could make a fortune!

In the early 1980s, I lived in what is sometimes referred to as a "transitional" neighborhood in Washington, D.C. For several years, I had the opportunity to observe the incessant, almost compulsive money-making routines of junkies. Day in and day out, these illiterate, uneducated, dirty, destitute, drugged-out, and degenerate creatures would go out into a very unfriendly world and hustle for money.

They begged. They pleaded. They panhandled. They stole. They ran card games and cons of every possible variety. And they made lots of money.

I read a longish article in the *Washington Post* at that time that said many of these jokers were making $300 to $400 a day to feed their habits.

That made an impression on me. I mean, hell, these guys were making more than I was. And I had two degrees and three jobs.

The more I thought about it, the more amazing it seemed to me. Here you have all these total life losers out there on the street making more money than a young journalist or a high-school teacher.

Very Impressive People

The fact that they were uneducated junkies didn't make their accomplishments any less impressive. Quite the contrary.

These were people whose primary goal in life was to *numb themselves into a stupor*. Yet they could go out into the unfriendly streets and earn two or three times the money I could inside a fancy, friendly office.

The more I thought about it, the more interested I became. I had a good idea of what a junkie did to earn his money. But I couldn't for the life of me figure out where he got the emotional strength to do it.

So I decided to start talking to some of my neighborhood junkies. They were easy to talk to. A dollar would buy a five-minute conversation. Five dollars and a cup of coffee could buy me five of them.

I eventually befriended three junkies. An old man named George who had once worked for the post office, a young man named Dean who had never worked a legitimate day in his life, and a mother of three named Desiree. At least that is what she told me her name was.

They all worked on 14th Street, which was the main corridor for hookers and drug addicts. It was also the crossroad I had to pass to get to Mrs. Phoenix's, the lady who took care of our eldest son while we were working downtown every day.

After dropping Number One Son (N1S) off at his babysitter's, I would spend a few minutes with George, Dean, or Desiree. I'd ask them casually about where they lived, when they slept, when they "worked," and so on.

Gradually, I figured out how they could make so much money every day. It wasn't some clever trick or con they were practicing (although they did have a few tricks they employed when they could). It was a combination of three very old-fashioned virtues.

Three Habits of Highly Successful Crackheads

1. George, Dean, and Desiree worked longer hours than I was working. I thought I was a hard worker because I worked 12 hours a day. These three worked every waking hour—which generally meant 18 to 20 hours a day.
2. Each of them worked with a single-minded purpose. Although they had occasional "kick-back" moments when they talked to me or nodded, 90 percent of their conscious time was focused on getting the money they needed to get their next fixes. I, by contrast, had a dozen interests and alternate ambitions that pulled me away from my job. But not them. They never diverted from their singular goals.
3. But the most important difference between George, Dean, Desiree, and me had to do with something deeper. Their addiction was much stronger than my ambition. And because of that, they would do *whatever it took* to get the money they needed.

If you study the lives of America's most successful people, you will discover that they too:

- Worked long and hard.
- Stayed focused on one goal.
- Made sacrifices to succeed.

Read the biography of Andrew Carnegie and you will see these three traits repeated throughout his life. Watch a documentary about Warren Buffett or Bill Gates and you will discover the same thing.

It's something to think about, isn't it?

Working long and hard is important to success. And having determination and focus is important, too. But to achieve really big goals . . . to climb into a whole new category . . . you have to do more.

If you took away his crack addiction, our illiterate young burger flipper could work as hard as he wanted . . . but he'd never make $600 a day. That can come only from the willingness to do whatever it takes, including things that are risky, uncomfortable, new, worrisome, or even dangerous.

Junkies don't get the respect they deserve.

Imagine what the addict's life is like. You wake up on a park bench smelling like urine. You stretch, rub the sores on your face and forearms, and say to yourself, "Up and at 'em, boy. Today you are going to go out there—to that cold and unfriendly city—and get your hands on six hundred bucks."

Could you do that? Day after day? I couldn't. Not unless I was addicted to something.

How to Tap into the Unappreciated Power of the Junkie

You can have the junkie's gift. And you don't even have to smoke crack to get it.

Somewhere inside you there is a fire burning. It's your core desire to be loved and appreciated. We all have it. And it is always very strong.

If you leave this fire alone, it will eventually burn itself out. Your life will slip by meaninglessly. When you die, your dreams will, too.

If you fan the flames of your core desire, the fire will grow. And that will mean one of two things: You will have the success you yearn for. Or you will do nothing, and the heat will scorch you from the inside out.

You have to find that burning desire inside you. And you have to use it to live your life.

It is damn hard to get a new venture going, to launch a new career, or to really break away from the past. It is difficult because it is different. And because it requires you to go beyond your comfort zone.

Take a look at your to-do list for today, as an example. There is probably something there you don't want to do. You know it is important. You have highlighted it. Yet, you are reluctant to do it.

Maybe it is making a difficult phone call. Or performing a tedious task. It is highly likely it is something you are not comfortable with.

That's why you haven't done it so far. And that's probably why your competitors haven't done it, either.

If you want to achieve more than you have ever achieved, you have to be willing to do more than you have ever done before. You need to commit yourself, put in the hours, stay focused, and, yes, do that unpleasant but very necessary task.

So do this right now. Pretend for a moment that you *are* a junkie and that getting your fix depends on accomplishing the one goal that escapes you. What—if your physical well-being depended on it—would you do to absolutely, positively (failure is not an option) succeed?

Set aside your qualms. Ignore your fears, at least for the moment. If nothing else mattered, what is it that you would do?

Got it? Good.

Now ask yourself: Why aren't you doing that?

Do you have a moral objection? A doubt? A fear of failing? Get those feelings out and take a hard look at them. That's what's keeping you from what you desire.

Face your feelings squarely. Think about how they are blocking you. If you do that fully and honestly today, you will have accomplished something important.

WHY POSITIVE THINKING DOESN'T WORK FOR MOST PEOPLE

One of the great fallacies in the self-help industry is the notion that you can change your life with "positive thinking."

The purveyors of positivism, starting with Napoleon Hill and including the people who now promote *The Secret*, contend that we all have, at our conscious disposal, the means to transform ourselves into walking, breathing success machines.

Some self-help gurus sell positive thinking because they know it is one of the most lucrative products to put in the marketplace. Change one thought and you can change your life! What better promise can you make to an underachieving, wanna-be-rich-and-successful couch potato?

And purely from a profit point of view, they are right. Positive thinking products making quick-and-easy promises account for more than a billion dollars a year in direct-mail and Internet sales. And that's just for the companies I personally know. The total number is probably multiples of that.

I am not saying all proponents of positive thinking are hucksters. Many are honest men and women who believe in the concept because they use it successfully in their own lives. They are usually people who have always been accomplished, excelling in sports or academics or business almost from the start. Their repeated successes gave them confidence that they can do just about anything. And they readily tap into that underlying feeling of confidence whenever they face a new challenge. In their hearts, they know they can succeed. So when they take on anything new, they can't help but believe they will be successful.

But what about the rest of the world? The 80 percent of the population that got Cs in school and sat on the bench during ball games and had little or no success in business? What messages are buried in their hearts?

Well, the positive thinkers will tell you that is exactly the point. The people who struggle on without success are failing because they don't really think they can succeed. If only they could change their thinking, they would do better.

And so the therapy for these self-doubters is positive thinking. Stand in front of the mirror in the morning and repeat 20 times: "I am a good person. I can do anything. I will be successful."

It's very appealing. Two or three minutes of talking to your mirrored image, and a mental switch will be turned. Everything after that will come to you effortlessly.

The reality is different.

Does Positive Thinking Work?

A study mentioned by Julie Norem in her book *The Positive Power of Negative Thinking* confirms my belief that, although positive thinking may work for people who already have an optimistic way of looking at their abilities, it doesn't work for people who are pessimists.

Researchers divided their subjects (all identified as pessimists) into two groups. They told one group that, based on their past performance, they were going to do well on a standardized test they were about to be given. And these subjects indicated on a pre-test survey that they did, indeed, feel optimistic about their results. The second group was not given any encouragement. The results? The first group, the temporarily optimistic pessimists, actually performed worse on the test.

I've been critical of the idea of positive thinking for years, because I think it is useless to the people who most need help in changing their lives: people who have deeply held negative *feelings* about what they can accomplish.

Positive thinking works only for those who are emotionally positive. Usually, these are people who have a history of being successful. People who have been good wrestlers, for example, find it easy to believe they will win their next wrestling match. Entrepreneurs like yours truly find it easy to believe their next business venture will be successful.

When you are *emotionally* positive, you can't help but *think* positively about everything.

So thinking positively helps. But it only helps the 20 percent of the population that is already emotionally positive. The rest of the population, the 80 percent of the world that is emotionally negative, cannot be helped by positive thinking.

I knew this was true, though I didn't know exactly why. When I wrote about it in the past, many *Early to Rise* readers objected. When I spoke about it at conferences, attendees complained to me afterward. They seemed angry. As if I were trying to take something precious away from them.

They believed I was trying to deny their best chance of succeeding. Meanwhile, what I was really trying to do was get them to stop conning themselves and take the specific actions that would help them achieve their goals.

As the years passed, I would meet some of these same people at other conferences. They were still attending self-improvement seminars, still carrying positive-thinking books, and still upset with me for telling them that positive thinking wouldn't change their fortunes. It had, after all, worked for the people promoting all those seminars and books.

Year after year. Decade after decade. They stayed poor. They stayed stuck. But they wouldn't give up their dream of changing their lives quickly and easily by changing their thinking.

I was never able to articulate why it was that I knew positive thinking would never work for these people. But then I read a book that helped me understand: *A General Theory of Love*. It was written by three eminent psychotherapists and neuroscientists. Let me tell you very briefly what it taught me that sheds light on this issue.

Essentially, our emotions are deeply rooted in the way our minds are wired. There is a scientific basis for many of our emotional responses and how we relate to others. At the same time, our interactions with the world and people around us have a profound impact on our attitude. This interaction, which can actually alter neural pathways in the brain, begins in infancy and influences our development.

So if you grew up with negative feelings about your ability to achieve success, that's the way your brain is wired. And no amount of positive thinking will change it.

Here is what the authors of *A General Theory of Love* (2001) have to say about the self-help industry:

> A vigorous self-help movement has championed the hoax that a strong-willed person, outfitted with the proper directions, can select good relationships. Those seduced into the promise of a quick fix gobble it up. But the physiology of emotional life cannot be dispelled with a few words . . .
>
>   . . . Self-help books are like car repair manuals: You can read them all day, but doing so doesn't fix a thing.

To change yourself from being emotionally negative to emotionally positive, you have to get some solid successes under your belt. And that's where another success technique—visualization—comes in. But this one works. Visualization is a proven and useful technique for achieving peak performance.

It's no secret that many of the most successful people in the world—including entertainers, athletes, and CEOs—used visualization to help them achieve their goals.

Take Michael Jordan . . .

> I visualized where I wanted to be, what kind of player I wanted to become. I knew exactly where I wanted to go, and I focused on getting there.

And Jack Nicklaus, one of the greatest golfers to ever grace the game, said, "I never hit a shot, not even in practice, without having a very sharp, in-focus picture of it in my head. It's like a color movie."

Famed sports psychologist Bob Rotella charges thousands of dollars per session to help pro athletes and business executives achieve success through visualization. In addition to coaching pro PGA golfers and top athletes in the NBA and NFL, he coaches high-ranking executives at Merrill Lynch, Morgan Stanley, General Electric, Coca-Cola, and many other companies.

Matt Furey, world-class martial artist and top Internet marketer, credits visualization for his success. Matt's wrestling coach told the scrawny, uncoordinated high-school teen he never had a chance. But by using the power of visualization, Matt gained the confidence to win match after match—and became a champion wrestler in high school and college.

Later, Matt became World Kung Fu Champion—thanks, again, to visualization and the very positive attitude that was now buried deep in his limbic brain (the part of the brain involved in emotional behavior).

As I said, people who are emotionally positive about their chances for success have a history of succeeding. They're *doers*, not dreamers. So forget about positive thinking. Instead, start rewiring your brain by working toward the goal you want to achieve or practicing the skill you want to master.

At first, you won't feel very good about what you're doing because you won't be very good at it. But stick with it. Remember that it takes about a thousand hours to achieve competency in anything that's worthwhile.

Start by setting very modest objectives. Use visualization to help you excel at specific tasks and overcome specific challenges. But don't waste your time repeating useless mantras. Actions—only actions—will reprogram your limbic brain and turn you into a real "success machine."

TOO SCARED TO TRY? A FORMULA FOR DEFEATING THE FEAR OF FAILURE

"I don't dance," Jane said to her cousin Ray as they watched an older couple dance at the wedding. "I've got two left feet. It's just too embarrassing."

"I used to be terrible," Ray said. "But then I took some lessons."

"I couldn't even take lessons," Jane said. "I'd be embarrassed to have the teacher see how bad I am."

"I know what you mean," Ray said. "I feel that way about golf."

I used to feel that way about public speaking. I dreaded the thought of it. And when I was forced to make a speech, I did a terrible job—which only made me dread the next speech even more. It was a vicious cycle.

When I became editorial director of a newsletter business in South Florida in 1982, I found myself in a position where I had to conduct meetings and give presentations at industry functions on a fairly regular basis—something I was ill-prepared to do. So I decided to enroll in a Dale Carnegie program for public speaking.

Somehow, I registered in the wrong course. Instead of focusing on speech making, it had a broader goal. And that program changed my life. It taught me the importance of goal setting and taking action. But it also, inadvertently, taught me to be more comfortable as a speaker.

My speech-making skills improved almost accidentally. Every week, we had to read a chapter of Carnegie's classic book, *How to Win Friends and Influence People*, and then come to class and make a two-minute presentation about how we were going to put the principle of that chapter to work in our lives.

On Thursday evenings after work, I would drive a half-hour to the place where we met. During that drive, I thought about what I was going to say. It was difficult in the beginning, but each week it got a little easier.

By the end of the 14-week course, I was performing at a near-professional level. I had won several awards in competition and was routinely rated at the top of the class. The final session was a sort of commencement ceremony. Relatives and friends were allowed to attend, which tripled the size of the audience we had to speak to. Everyone did pretty well, as I remember. I gave the last speech. I was still a little nervous when I got up to the podium, but I had learned a lot by then. So I took a deep breath and did my thing.

I got a strong round of applause. Several people I didn't even know came up to congratulate me, and one suggested I should become a comedian. I wasn't foolish enough to take his advice to heart, but it did make me happy to think that I had made so much progress in so little time, starting from practically zero.

How did I conquer my fear of public speaking? The same way you would conquer the fear of anything else.

So, What Are You Afraid Of?

There are entire systems of psychotherapy devoted to curing people of their fears. The most effective are those that gradually expose the phobic person to whatever it is that they're afraid of. If you feared snakes, for example, the treatment might begin with looking at photographs of snakes. Then, once you were comfortable with that, you might move on to watching videotapes of snakes. And then on to looking at snakes in cages . . . and then looking at them uncaged but at a distance . . . and then, gradually, getting closer until you could actually handle them without emotional discomfort.

Likewise, if you were afraid of public speaking, the therapy would be to make a very short speech in front of a very small audience and then to gradually expose yourself to longer speeches and bigger audiences until you were comfortable speaking for an hour or more in front of a large number of people.

That was what happened to me. The Dale Carnegie course I took turned out to be a therapeutic program of graduated exposure therapy to public speaking.

Fears of specific things—snakes, public speaking, flying, and so on—can be overcome with *gradual exposure*. But what about more general fears . . . like the fear of failing?

To answer that question, we've got to figure out what, exactly, we are afraid of when we say we are afraid of failing.

Imagine that you are alone in a quiet room trying to solve a difficult crossword puzzle. You can't do it.

How do you feel?

Now imagine yourself competing in a national crossword puzzle championship. It is down to four finalists—you and three others. The four of you are standing up on a stage in front of large puzzles with markers in your hand. Six hundred people in the audience and millions more on TV are watching you. The timekeeper gives the signal, and you are off, filling out the answers as fast as you can. Before you have finished one-sixth of your puzzle, the first winner is declared. Before you have finished a quarter of it, the second winner has rung in. Now it is just you and one opponent. You are halfway done and feeling hope-ful. Then you hear the buzzer. He has finished well ahead of you. You are standing there with your marker in your hand. The other three contestants are smiling.

How do you feel this time?

When I tried this little experiment, I had two distinctly different emotions. Imagining the first scenario made me feel a little angry. Imagining the second one made me feel embarrassed.

In the first scenario, I am just an ordinary puzzle solver playing an ordinary game. I fail to accomplish my goal, but I am not embar-rassed. In the second scenario, I am a national-caliber puzzle solver. I fail . . . but in front of a large audience. This adds shame to my anger. And that feels much worse.

So perhaps we can say this about the fear of failing: A big part of what we are afraid of is embarrassment—being shamed in front of other people.

Humiliation and Humility

When embarrassment is extreme, we call it humiliation. If you pass gas at a fancy dinner party, you feel embarrassed. If your big project at work fails miserably—and you've been bragging that it would be a "sure thing," you feel humiliated.

Humiliation is what happens to embarrassment when it is mixed with pride. The prouder you are, the more failure hurts.

Which brings us to our cure for the fear of failure: humility.

I'm guilty of pride myself. I'm proud of my writing, for example, and the success I've had in business. So I have to keep reminding myself to be humble about those things. But I am not proud of everything I do. I take no pride in my ability to dance or to sing or to speak foreign languages, because I do those things so badly. And because my ego isn't involved, I am not embarrassed to ask stupid questions, to show myself as a beginner, and ultimately to fail again and again as I attempt to master those skills.

The truth is, when I started out in business, I wasn't very good at that, either. Again, that made it possible for me to ask lots of questions, look stupid, and make mistakes . . . which accelerated my learning curve.

The Secret of Accelerated Failure

That last observation brings us to an important principle of success. I call it "the secret of accelerated failure."

The principle of accelerated failure is this: To develop any complex skill, you must be willing to make mistakes and endure failures. The faster you can make those mistakes and suffer those failures, the quicker you will master the skill.

At ETR, we teach this secret to our managers. We encourage them to allow their employees to fail. Not to fail stupidly. Not to make the same mistakes over and over again. But to feel free to fail at something so long as it was done in the pursuit of knowledge.

If you play golf or practice jujitsu, you know this to be true. If you tense up and focus on avoiding mistakes, you will learn very slowly. If you relax, let the mistakes happen, and learn from them, you will advance quickly.

It starts with being humble. Humble enough to accept the fact that when you begin anything new, you are likely to do it poorly.

Humility Is Nature's First Gift

Pride prevents us from admitting we are incompetent. But we are all incompetent when we're learning.

Think of how a baby learns to walk. He begins by crawling and then advances to "forward falling" (as my brother calls it), and then to walking like a little drunk, and finally to walking masterfully. Babies don't feel shame because they are not proud. There is a reason that pride does not invade the human psyche until six or seven years of age. There is simply too much to learn before then. If toddlers had pride, it would take them years or even decades to walk and talk properly.

Humility is a much underrated virtue. It provides us with at least three significant advantages:

1. **It makes us more endearing.** Humble people—especially accomplished individuals who remain humble—are well liked.
2. **It makes it easier to get cooperation.** Humble people get more cooperation from others, because they don't try to force strong-minded people to accept their ideas.

3. **It makes it easier and faster to learn.** Humble people are able to ask questions, make mistakes, and experience failure without embarrassment. This attracts good people to them who want to help. Humble people get the best teachers and get the most from their teachers.

If Humility Is the Solution, How Does a Proud Person Become Humble?

Now we are coming to the most important part of this discussion— a practical plan for defeating the fear of failure. Here's how you can do it:

1. **Begin by accepting the truth.** You are a good person, but that doesn't mean you are naturally good at everything. Look in the mirror and think about the skill you want to accomplish. Say out loud, "I accept the fact that right now I am incompetent at (name the skill)." Repeat this exercise until it doesn't hurt.

2. **Admit your incompetence to an indifferent audience.** Once you can say it in front of a mirror, say it in front of a living human being. Begin by admitting your incompetence to someone who doesn't care. Admit to your Spanish teacher that you are incompetent at public speaking. Admit to your public-speaking coach that you are incompetent at speaking Spanish. Repeat this exercise until you can do it with grace and good humor.

3. **Admit your incompetence to a judgmental audience.** Admit that you are no good at languages to your Spanish teacher. Admit that you have two left feet to your dance instructor. Do this not once, but every time you make a mistake or fail in some way. Do it with grace and good humor. As pop psychologists say, "own" the feeling.

4. **Admit your incompetence to someone who can punish you.** This is the ultimate test. The next time you volunteer for a difficult assignment at work, admit to your boss that you might fail before you succeed. Do it with grace and good humor and you will be amazed at the result. Your boss won't

can you on the spot. (Unless he is *really* incompetent.) Rather, he will admire you for your humility. After all, he knows you are not yet competent. All he wants is your commitment to carry on until you are.

I've found that the most productive and successful executives are very comfortable about saying, "I'm going to try such and such. I'll probably screw it up completely. But if I eventually succeed . . . just think what good will come of it!"

That's what you want for your company. That's what you want for yourself. Defeat your fear of failure by being happy—and even eager—to try and fail until you finally succeed. That's how Edison invented the light bulb. That's how Michael Jordan, a very mediocre basketball player in high school, became the greatest hoops player of all time. They weren't afraid of failure. You shouldn't be, either.

HOW TO BECOME WHAT YOU WANT TO BE

"If you want to be a writer, you have to write."

I was 16 years old when my father said those kind—and cruel— words to me. I never forgot them.

The first time I can remember *wanting to be a writer*, I was 11 or 12 years old. I'd written a poem for Sister Mary Something at school. My rhyming quatrain (AABB) was titled, pretentiously, "How Do I Know the World Is Real?"

I was at the kitchen table when my father started reading it over my shoulder. I felt anxious. My father was a credentialed writer, an award-winning playwright, a Shakespearean scholar, and a teacher of literature, including poetry. I'd seen him, on Saturday mornings, hunched over student essays, muttering and occasionally reading aloud passages to my mother that sounded perfectly good to me but elicited derisive laughter from them.

My father understood the secret-to-me clues of *good writing*. I didn't feel at all comfortable having my fragile young poem exposed to the awesome danger of his critical mind. So there I sat, hoping he would go away. But he didn't. I felt his hand on my shoulder, gentle and warm. "You may have a talent for writing," he said.

I wrote lots of poetry in the months that followed, and began to think of myself as a writer. I liked that feeling. But soon other interests—touch football, the Junior Police Club, girls—crowded themselves into my life. Gradually, I wrote less and less. I still yearned *to be a writer* and so I began to feel guilty about not writing.

To assuage my guilt, I promised myself that my other activities were "life experience" and that I needed life experience to become the good writer I wanted to be. In developing this excuse for not writing, I was building a structure of self-deception that many people live inside when they abandon their dreams. From the outside, it looks like you are doing nothing. But from the inside, you know that you are in the process of *becoming*, which, you convince yourself, is the next best thing to *being*.

That was the shape of my delusion when my father said, "If you want to be a writer, you have to write. A writer is someone who writes."

So many people live their lives failing to become what they want to be because they can't find the time to get started. How many times have you heard someone say that, one day, they will do what they always wanted to do—travel the world or paint paintings or write a book? And when you hear sentiments like those, what do you feel? Happy, because you are confident that one day they will accomplish their long-held goal? Or sort of sad for them, because you are pretty sure they never will?

And what about you? What is it that you want to be but haven't become? What goal or project or task do you keep talking about accomplishing yet never do?

When my father told me that "writers write," he was saying two things:

1. I had lost the right to call myself a writer when I stopped writing.
2. I could regain the title the moment I started writing again.

If you spend a while ruminating on this, you may find it both disturbing and liberating.

I was disturbed, because I wanted my father to say that the way to become a writer was to read books about writing and then take courses on writing and then perhaps become an apprentice to a writer and then begin writing little bits here and there. And that, finally, after 3 or 10 years of education, preparation, and qualification, I would somehow automatically be a writer.

But as long as I was studying writing or preparing myself to be a writer—and yet not actually writing—I wasn't a writer. It was as simple as that.

Lots of people feel that they can keep their dreams alive and derive some of the ego satisfaction they hope their dreams will give them simply by living in a state of becoming. "I am not yet the person I want to become, but so long as I continue to express a wish to become that person, I keep that possibility alive and deserve credit for doing so."

To become a writer, the first thing I had to do was refuse to accept any psychological credit for wanting to be a writer. After the initial disappointment of giving up the delusion that *becoming* was as good as *being*, I had no choice but to jump over the becoming stage and simply *be*.

I did that by writing. Every day. And when I learned the secret of getting up early and writing first thing in the morning—hours before other people trailed into work—that's when I began to really live my dream.

These days, I fire up the computer in my home office by 7:30 each morning. There is no better feeling than to get going first thing, usually by making entries into my journal, but sometimes by tackling something tougher, like a book chapter. Of the many pleasures of being a writer—finishing a manuscript, collaborating with editors, seeing a copy of the book for the first time, and even making it to bestseller lists—the purest and finest for me has always been the first few hours of the morning when I am in that writerly groove.

The best part about being a writer, I have discovered, is the writing. (It is also the worst part, but that's another story.) And this is true, I think, for every skill or profession.

The easiest way to become something special is also the fastest: Just start doing it. Don't wait for the "right" time. Don't worry about not being qualified. And don't worry about getting paid for it. Just start doing it.

You want to become a musician? Start playing that piano.

You want to become a philanthropist? Start investing your money.

You want to become a basketball player? Start shooting those hoops.

Don't spend another minute talking about what you will do . . . one day.

WHEN TO DOUBT YOURSELF

Gurus of success often speak of self-doubt as if it were a damning trait. Inspirational author Wayne Dyer put it this way in his book *Your Sacred Self: Making the Decision to Be Free*: "Keep in mind always that doubt is produced by your ego. Doubt is not a part of your higher spiritual self. With this awareness you can learn to observe your doubt rather than choose to own it. . . . Then observe how doubt literally forces you to act in predetermined and limited ways."

In fact, questioning your ability to accomplish a desired goal is a healthy and intelligent way to begin any challenging objective, especially so when that objective is your career. Unbridled optimism in the face of near-impossible or impossible odds is another term for foolishness. If you want to lead a life of maximum accomplishment and minimum heartache, you should adopt an approach to challenge that is one part confidence, one part caution, and one part enthusiasm.

I met a 50-something-year-old woman at a seminar recently who told me that she was going to create a million-dollar business in five years by writing and illustrating poems. If her financial target weren't crazy enough to give her pause, her business goal should have been. And if her business goal weren't bonkers enough, a modest assessment of her writing skills (she showed me one of her poems) should have cooled her down.

When I suggested that, before committing to this career change, she study the children's book market and/or read my book *Seven Years to Seven Figures*, she looked at me as if I had slapped her. "Don't you believe in positive thinking?" she asked.

"I believe, *positively*, in thinking," I said. And I left it at that.

To give yourself the best chance of achieving the possible, the right mental mix is a clear, focused, and conscious ambition based on knowing a good deal about both yourself and the thing you are trying to do.

And that starts with asking some tough questions:

- Is my goal realistic? Has it ever been done before? If so, how often? How often has it been tried unsuccessfully? What are the statistical odds of succeeding?
- Do I have what it takes? Do I have the intelligence? The capacity to learn? The emotional stamina to succeed?

On this subject, Sheila, an *Early to Rise* reader who also is a middle-aged woman, writes:

I had an assignment 35 years ago to write a short story and submit the manuscript to a publisher for a grade in my Children's Literature class. I didn't receive favorable results and gave up my dream of writing stories for children.

I am now retired, [and] the urge to write is stronger than ever. What steps should I take to determine if I have any talent or should leave it alone?

Kudos for Sheila. Her career ambition, thwarted by a single negative review when she was younger, has resurfaced, and she has the good sense to ask this sensible question before leaping forward.

Doubt is not the opposite of faith; it is one element of faith.
—*Paul Tillich*

The short answer to her question is this: Based on the little sample of writing her note provided, I believe she does have the raw talent to write short stories for children. Writing is a skill that can be learned. Writing stories for children is a special skill, the techniques of which are available in many books and programs.

To learn that skill, Sheila will need to devote between 600 and 1,000 hours to such books and programs. But before she does that, she should make a frank assessment of her chances of making any kind of decent money as an author of children's books, and whether she is financially prepared to devote several years to this process without any financial recompense.

Finally, she must imagine herself spending four or five hours of every day sitting alone and tapping on a keyboard. If she hasn't spent any time doing that since college, then she might want to take a week of days right now to see if the actual, quotidian experience of writing is as rewarding as she has been imagining.

Talking to professional children's book writers is a good preliminary step to take. In a few short hours of casual conversation, Sheila can benefit from the experience of people who have done what she wants to do.

None of what I am saying right now should stop Sheila from becoming a story writer for children. All of the aforementioned advice was meant to answer her question—which was about assessing her chances of getting the skills she needs to make her dream into a career.

If Sheila's goal is simply to become a writer of children's stories, she should start writing them immediately. She should study the guides as she goes, but the ultimate learning will take place with the writing. And the writing can begin right now—even before she is sure she wants to make writing a career rather than just a beloved avocation.

Sheila should keep in mind a point I've made many times: You can't become something, such as a writer, by studying to be it. You become that thing the moment you start doing it every day. If Sheila starts writing children's stories today and keeps on writing them for a year, next year at this time she will be not only better at the writing, she will be able to call herself a writer.

TAKING THE BIG LEAP

Sometime in your business career, you will have a chance to do something or sell something—and it will be obvious to you that you are looking at a great opportunity. However, you will realize that you simply don't have the time, the knowledge, or the resources to meet that challenge. If you are sensible, you will probably say "No thanks," and bow out. But—if the opportunity is really extraordinary—you might want to try the Grand Canyon Jump.

I'm thinking of Robbie Knievel's now-famous motorcycle jump over the Grand Canyon. (Robbie Knievel is the son of legendary daredevil Evel Knievel.) The story I heard was that the idea was based on his father's failed attempt at the same stunt.

I remember one of the very first times I took a "Grand Canyon Jump"—albeit in a much less bold way. It was more than 10 years ago.

Early to Rise was brand-new, and I was still learning how to apply my direct-marketing background to the Internet. I got an invitation to speak at a seminar about Internet marketing. Trouble was, I knew next to nothing about the subject. Certainly not enough to make a speech about it. (Number One Rule of Effective Speaking: Know what you're talking about.)

But I agreed to make the presentation because I figured it would force me to think about this important and growing part of my business. Not only did I agree to talk, I agreed to a title for my speech ("7 Myths About the Internet and 7 Ways to Profit from It") that was—given my experience at the time—audacious.

Since then, I have made the leap many times. (This is what's behind my "Ready, Fire, Aim" philosophy.)

When I really want to do something but have no idea how to do it, I don't just agree to do it—I promise myself that I will do it very well. I set a high hurdle for myself. I suppose what I'm doing is fueling my drive with the fear of humiliation.

And it works. Most of the time.

In the case of my "7 Myths About the Internet" speech, I pushed myself because I had to. By reading about what others have done. Observing what my own employees were doing—what was working and what was failing miserably. Trying some stuff on my own. And I made remarkable progress. In fact, after only two months, I had gotten to the point where 80 percent of what I read about Internet marketing either bored me because it was so simple or infuriated me because it was so obviously wrong.

As the weeks passed and the day of the presentation grew nearer, I found myself thinking harder about the subject. More than ever, I was aware of how other media I was well-versed in (direct mail, print advertising, and so forth) reminded me of the Internet. Bit by bit, ideas were coming together.

When the event finally took place, I had come up with about a dozen useful ideas and observations that felt right. Many of these defied conventional wisdom. Then, when I heard what other presenters were saying—their accounts of what succeeded and failed for them—it all made sense.

My presentation worked. It felt good. I was full of energy when I gave it, thinking, "Hey, this really is important!" And I got a good reaction from the audience. Most important, I got what I hoped to get: a foundation of ideas that have helped me—and will continue to help me—make money on the Internet.

These days, trying to do anything in addition to holding onto your job may seem like an enormous challenge. And rightly so. But that's all the more reason to make the Grand Canyon Jump.

Think about one thing that you have not done or declined to do that could be very good for your career long-term. It could be something general, like learning how to sell on the Internet . . . or something more specific, like making your next sales presentation or pay-per-click campaign work.

Next step is to announce your intention. Contact the appropriate parties and let them know what you've decided to do.

Finally, set a high standard for yourself. Set the standard so high that it seems foolish or pretentious—and then start thinking about how you can actually achieve it.

You can't change the laws of physics. Robbie Knievel jumped over a "narrow" segment of the Grand Canyon rather than going for its widest section. But he got over it. And it gave him not only the temporary career boost he was looking for but also a stunt that he will always be remembered for.

So what's it going to be? When—and how—are you going to make your Grand Canyon Jump?

CHECKING YOUR PROGRESS

One of the most important actions you can take when you are master planning your life is to monitor where you have been and where you are. This simple step can help you achieve practically any goal you have set for yourself.

Take your health, for instance. If you want to lose weight, keeping track of your progress can actually help you accomplish that goal.

Fitness expert Craig Ballantyne pointed me to a study by researchers from Brown Medical School and Drexel University. The objective of the study was to determine whether consistent "weighing in" would affect weight maintenance.

At the end of the year, the subjects who weighed themselves every day lost more weight and kept more weight off than those who weighed themselves less frequently. "Consistently monitoring yourself after you've lost weight," Craig noted, "is clearly a key component of keeping it off."

That reminded me of a recommendation I made in my book *Automatic Wealth*. If your goal is to become wealthy, I pointed out, it's a good idea to track your net worth on a regular basis. I said:

> I believe that most successful money-makers regularly count their money . . . they regularly assess their fortunes. As their net income grows and they feel more comfortable with their wealth and more confident of their income, they count less. When they get super-wealthy—Warren Buffett wealthy—they don't have to count their money. *Fortune* magazine and countless other entities do it for them. But on their way up, they count. And that's what I recommend you do.
>
> Specifically, I suggest that you do a personal balance sheet every month. Create a spreadsheet that lists all your assets and all your debts. Include valuable possessions, stocks, bonds, mutual funds, gold, real estate (aside from your home), and so forth.
>
> You'll be amazed at how much this simple commitment can affect the way you think and even the way you act.

I've come across studies that found the same thing to be true of goal setting in general: If you write down your goals and check them regularly, you'll have a much better chance of achieving them.

For instance, a recent study from DayTimer.com concluded that American workers with the highest incomes and most success in the workplace are those who have written goals. These superstars also have the habit of writing daily task lists prioritized in a way to help them achieve those goals. On the flip side, of the more than 70 percent of workers who don't write down career or financial goals, only 9 percent accomplish what they set out to do each day.

So those are three things you should be checking regularly:

- Your weight (or, better yet, body-fat composition).
- Your net worth.
- Your progress toward your life goals.

Get on it!

Part Six

SKILLS OF THE MOST SUCCESSFUL

WHY YOU CAN LEARN SO MUCH FROM A MENTOR

A man looks back on his life and says, "I wish I knew then what I know now."

It can take a decade or more to become the successful person you want to be, but you can shorten your learning curve—even drastically curtail it—by using a mentor.

With the advice, experience, and support of an experienced person in your field, you can avoid the most common mistakes you are likely to make.

You overcome the stickiest problems and find shortcuts to success!

It doesn't really matter where you are along your career path; getting yourself a good mentor will be enormously valuable for you . . .

A survey commissioned by the Elliot Leadership Institute at Johnson & Wales University confirms this.

For this particular study, researchers surveyed senior executives and middle managers in the food service and hospitality industries about leadership competencies.

What they discovered was that leaders who had been mentored felt the experience invaluable. They said their mentors helped them build all kinds of leadership skills, including decision making, strategic thinking, planning, coaching, and effectively managing others.

When it comes to mentors, I always look to those in my own business life.

From Leo, my first post-college boss, I learned the importance of persistence and dogged determination.

Leo once had me call Honda Motors more than 100 times to convince them to give us a new engine after the one we had died (from lack of oil).

We hadn't a single, sensible argument in our favor, but that didn't stop Leo from pushing me.

Finally, after I got all the way to the top, the Honda executive leadership decided they had wasted too much time on us and gave in!

I didn't feel good about getting something we didn't deserve, but I never forgot that lesson in persistence.

From Joel, my second major mentor, I learned a great deal.

The first lesson he taught me—by firing the woman who wanted to get me fired—was that a good leader needs to surround himself with the strongest people he can find.

Another lesson I learned soon thereafter had to do with the fundamental nature of business. "Until you make a sale," Joel explained patiently, "nothing else happens."

From Bill, a client, partner, and part-time mentor, I discovered—relatively late in my career—two important business secrets that have made me a better leader.

For one thing, I no longer feel compelled to solve every problem put at my feet. I've watched Bill ignore countless squabbles and come out much the better for it.

Before getting involved in a dispute these days, I ask myself, "Can these people eventually come up with a satisfactory solution themselves?"

If the answer is affirmative, I do nothing.

Thanks to Bill, I'm also now a big believer in product quality.

Having mastered the secrets of selling through my relationship with Joel, I tended to underestimate the importance of the product.

I was one of those marketers who actually wanted to sell snow to Eskimos!

In working with Bill—whose sole focus is always on quality—I've seen how much better a business becomes when you stress quality.

You probably have no idea what you need to learn to make the next leap forward in your career . . .

But someone who's been there and done it before does.

Getting the help of that person will make a very big difference in your future.

How to Find the Right Mentor for You

Look around your industry to find five successful business leaders who retired within the past two to five years.

This two- to five-year time frame is important.

If they've been retired for any longer, they could be out of touch. Any sooner, and they're not yet bored enough with retirement to miss thinking about work.

Write each of these five people a short letter expressing genuine admiration for their careers. Compliment them on specific achievements.

Then ask for advice on your own career.

Offer an invitation to go to lunch. Or, if they're located out of your local area, ask for a 15-minute phone call.

And don't—I repeat, don't—offer them any compensation for their help . . . yet.

Odds are, at least one of the five will respond positively to your invitation and give you a little of his time.

If you find that you get along, you've got yourself a mentor.

WHAT DANCING CAN TEACH YOU ABOUT LEADERSHIP

The three most important lessons in leadership I ever learned, I learned on the dance floor.

About a dozen years ago, K and I decided to do something about our fear of dancing at social events. We hired a ballroom dance instructor to teach us the basics: one slow dance, one fast dance, and a rudimentary salsa.

It was a simple goal, and we made quick progress when we were learning the footwork side by side. But when our instructor had us join hands and dance together, all hell broke loose. K had her ideas about how we should move, and I had mine.

Within minutes, the dance we were attempting to do would turn into a Greco-Roman wrestling match—she would pull me one way, while I pushed her another way. Our instructor tried to solve the problem by asking us to dance more smoothly. When that didn't work, he sat us down and gave us a little lecture.

"Dancing," he said, "is a partnership. But it's a partnership where the man leads, and the woman follows."

He looked at K. She was glaring at him.

"I know you don't like to follow," he said. "But if you want to dance well together, you are going to have to do it."

You can imagine the look on my face when he said that. As hard as I tried, I could not suppress a huge grin. Yes, in ballroom dancing—even these days—the man leads. This is a flagrant contradiction—not only of the way a good marriage operates, but also of common sense. After all, most women can dance a little. And most men look (and feel) ridiculous the moment they start.

No matter. Tradition rules on the dance floor. You may move more like Steve Martin in *The Jerk* than Fred Astaire, but if you are the man, then you are in charge of the dance.

"It usually comes as a shock," our instructor explained. "But if you stick with it, it can work."

It was quite a trial for K. She almost broke down several times during the following 30 minutes. "I don't think I can do this!" she said in a voice that sent chills down my spine.

"Learning to follow," our instructor said sympathetically, "is not easy. It's a skill. And for some people, a difficult one. For one thing, you have to do the same thing your partner is doing, except backward. Just as important, you have to follow his lead, even if it seems as if he's going the wrong way."

That barely satisfied K. "Why can't he learn to dance backward?" she said.

Our instructor smiled at her. "Do you really think he is capable of that?"

"I guess not," she said.

"And if he learns to lead well," he promised, "you may actually enjoy the feeling of being led."

"Yeah, right," K said. But she did her best to follow. It wasn't long before our instructor stopped us again and gave us lecture number two.

"Being a leader doesn't mean pushing your partner around," he said to me sternly. "Leading is all about sensitivity. And you, Mr. Masterson, have so far showed very little of that."

Now it was K's turn to smile.

I defended myself as glibly as I could. "Sensitivity," I said, "is one quality I have always eschewed. I once thought I should write a book for men like me titled *30 Days to Complete Insensitivity*."

Our instructor was not amused. He crossed his arms in front of his chest and shook his head slowly, looking at me the way you might look at your dog after he has just peed on the carpet.

"It is impossible to lead well if you're shoving your partner around. You will look like a thug, and she will not enjoy dancing with you at all. To lead well, you need to know exactly where your partner is at every moment. You have to know what foot her weight is balanced on without looking. You have to know her pacing, her strengths, and her weaknesses. And you have to take all that into consideration every time you move with her in your arms."

"Can you put that in writing and have him sign it in blood?" K wanted to know.

"It will take some time," our instructor replied. "But I believe we can turn this ox into a leader if he is just willing to follow three rules."

I was, I have to admit, interested to hear what those three rules were. They turned out to be very simple and yet very powerful. They made me a better dancer immediately. But more important, they later helped me understand how to be a better business leader, too.

Here are the three rules:

1. Know What You Are Going to Do Before You Do It

On the dance floor: "One big mistake men often make on the dance floor," our instructor said, "is that they make split-second decisions about which move they want to do next. That gives them no time at all to signal their partner, so they compensate by pushing and shoving. Pushing and shoving is the opposite of good dancing. And it's easy to avoid. Just know what your next step is going to be, and give your partner the signal at the right time so she can follow you gracefully."

To demonstrate how bad I was at leading, our instructor videotaped me run through a salsa by myself, pretending to have K in my arms. He played it back for us and pointed out how jerky my movements were. "You look that way because you're waiting too long before you decide what your next step is going to be. If you look awkward dancing alone, you can imagine how awkward you'll look as a couple, when she's trying to follow your last-minute movements."

In business: Having a long-term vision of what your business should become is like knowing what type of dance you want to do. But being a good leader requires more of you than that. It demands that you also have good ideas about the medium- and short-term tasks that are required to achieve that vision. And it means you have to communicate those ideas to your partners—the employees, vendors, and suppliers who are working closely with you to achieve your long-term vision.

2. Signal Your Intentions Distinctly

On the dance floor: To develop my first leading skill, I practiced our three dances by myself until I had a complete repertoire of moves I could do without making any quick or sudden changes. Then K and I resumed dancing together.

It was much better, but there were still problems. Every once in a while, K hesitated or stumbled. I thought, "Gee, I must be learning faster than she is." Our instructor had another interpretation. "You are not leading well," he told me.

"But I know what I am going to do," I protested. "And I'm giving her the signals."

"I don't think so," he said. And then he had me dance with him.

Our instructor was a big, burly sort of guy. Were I inclined to dance with men, I would not be jumping to sign his dance card. Still, I did the best I could and tried to lead him flawlessly.

After just a few turns, he stopped me and said, "Just as I expected. You are not giving your signals strongly enough."

"Huh?" I said. "I thought you didn't want me to use force."

"Right," he replied. "And the way to avoid using force is to give strong, clear signals."

He demonstrated by having me dance with him leading. I could feel my testosterone plunging as I dutifully obliged, K grinning happily as she watched.

What I noticed was that our instructor's signals—various sorts of touches on the back—were imperceptible to anyone watching but were very obvious to me because they were, as he had said, strong and clear.

"You can't follow well if your leader is giving you wishy-washy signals," he explained. "The stronger your signals are, the easier it is to follow you. And the easier it is for your partner to follow you, the better you'll look and the better she'll like dancing with you."

In business: Knowing what you want from your partners (again, your employees and vendors and suppliers) is not enough. You have to let them know what you want them to do by communicating it to them very clearly. And you have to give them enough time to do it.

3. Lead to Demonstrate Your Partner's Strengths

On the dance floor: For the next several lessons, I worked diligently at making my signals clearer and more distinct. And sure enough, K's occasional missteps, which I had been attributing to her, all but ceased. But there was still one more lesson I had to learn before our instructor would deem me a "good leader."

"You have come a long way," he told me one day after we had performed our three dances reasonably gracefully. "But there is one more thing that you need to do—and this will take you to the next level."

We were eager to find out what that one thing was. I sort of expected it to be some sort of fancy footwork or something about body posture or timing.

"I can think of three turns that K does especially well," he told me. "But I don't see her making those turns very often. What I see most of are the moves you like to do, Mr. Masterson." And then he just stared at me.

I felt, once again, like a dog that had peed on the carpet. I tucked my metaphorical tail between my legs and asked, "But isn't it natural to do what you like to do?"

"It's natural, but it's wrong," he said. "In dancing, the purpose of the man is to lead—but the purpose of the dance itself is to showcase the woman."

"Think of Fred Astaire," he said, "one of the greatest dancers that ever lived. None of the women he danced with had his level of mastery. But he always made them look better than they were and put them at the center of the dance when they were performing the moves they did best."

When he explained it that way, this rule made perfect sense. And by keeping it in mind, I was able to improve my dancing almost immediately.

In business: If you want all your business efforts to be successful, you need to get all your partners (once again, your employees and vendors and suppliers) working at their peak levels. And you want to take full advantage of all the things they do especially well—which means giving them the opportunity to do those things (especially when they're better at them than you are).

All three lessons are critically important—in fact, necessary—for good leadership. But this third one is the most important for business leaders whose businesses are beyond the first stage of development—in other words, when continued business growth demands the contributions of many talented people, not just the energy and genius of the entrepreneur who started things going. (I explain the various stages of business development in detail in my book *Ready, Fire, Aim*.)

Being a good leader means you have to have a vision. It means you have to have a plan, too, so your partners know what their next steps should be. It means communicating those next steps with precision and in time for them to respond. And it means giving your partners the space they need to do their own thing.

THE POWER OF A SIMPLE QUESTION

After hearing a news report about the Beatles phenomenon in England, 15-year-old Marsha Albert wrote to her local Washington, D.C., radio station and asked, "Why can't we have music like that here in America?"

Inspired by Marsha's question, disk jockey Carroll James managed to get a copy of "I Want to Hold Your Hand" from a British flight attendant and introduced the song to his WWDC radio audience on December 17, 1963.

Within minutes, requests for the record flooded the station. Within days, radio stations all across the United States were playing the song. And Capital Records was forced to release it on December 26, three weeks earlier than scheduled.

It is not the answer that enlightens, but the question.

—*Decouvertes*

According to Bruce Spizer, author of *The Beatles Are Coming! The Birth of Beatlemania in America*, when the band appeared on Ed Sullivan's TV show on February 9, 1964, 73 million people—an unprecedented 40 percent of the U.S. population at the time—watched.

"There's no doubt whatsoever that the Beatles would have conquered America anyway," Beatles historian Martin Lewis told *USA Today*. "But the speed and magnitude of that stratospheric kick-off could not have happened without Marsha Albert. If the record had been released on January 13th, as planned, kids wouldn't have heard it 20 times a day, as they did during the school break. It would never have sold one million copies in three weeks. There wouldn't have been 10,000 kids at JFK to greet the Beatles. Marsha didn't start Beatlemania. She jump-started it."

That's what a single, simple question can do.

Think about the couples who might never have met and gotten married had it not been for that old, reliable question: "Is someone sitting here?"

Think about the chances you might have missed in your own life by failing to ask "Can I?" Or "Would you?" Or "Is he?"

In 1982, I was working at a dead-end journalism job for a small Washington, D.C., publishing house. I knew it was time to get a move on if I didn't want to end up bored silly and making a meager living for the rest of my life. But I wasn't sure what to do.

As it happened, K had planned a week's vacation for us in Key Largo, where her brother worked for a Jet Ski rental business. Since we were going to be in Florida anyway, I figured I'd schedule a few job interviews. Not because I was hopeful of finding a good job there, but because I wanted to write off the travel expenses as a tax deduction.

I had two possible leads. One was a colleague, a high-ranking editor at the *Washington Post* who, I figured, might know someone in Florida.

The other was the name and address of a publisher in Boca Raton, Florida, who had been sending me promotions for his newsletters.

But to pursue these leads, I would have to ask questions—which is something I've always been reluctant to do, especially if the answer could be something I didn't want to hear.

But I did it.

I asked the *Washington Post* editor, "Do you know anybody in Florida who might give me a job interview?" And I wrote to the Boca Raton publisher and asked, "Do you have a place in your organization for a person like me?"

As a result, by the time K and I left for our vacation, I had three job interviews lined up. One was with the editor-in-chief of the *St. Petersburg Times*. Another was with a news editor for the *Miami Herald*. And the third one was with Joel, the newsletter publisher in Boca Raton.

I met with each one of these guys en route. And by the time we reached Key Largo, I had three job offers. Getting three offers out of three interviews was an astonishing thing. And it left me with a dilemma.

Should I take the high road that might lead to a Pulitzer Prize and everlasting fame as a respected journalist? Or the low road—journalistic obscurity but with the implied promise of a Big Bag of Gold for my efforts?

Which one should I choose?

The only person who could really answer that question was me. But that didn't stop me from soliciting opinions from even the most unlikely sources, including a 17-year-old pothead whose job in life was to refill the Jet Skis with gasoline.

After I told him my long story, he paused, took a toke on his joint, and said, "Go Boca."

Turns out that, after much soul-searching, I came to the same conclusion. And that decision was the trigger for all of the good things I have since accomplished.

But it all started when I forced myself to ask a few influential people the right questions at the right time.

DOUBLE YOUR PERSONAL POWER BY MASTERING ONE SKILL

In any organization, power moves inexorably to those who have mastered the art of persuasion. Whether you express yourself online, on the phone, or in person doesn't matter much. What counts is your ability to convince people that your ideas are worthwhile.

Think about the world's richest and most inspiring people. Think about Warren Buffett, Oprah Winfrey, Barack Obama. Yes, they have intelligence, ambition, and good instincts. And, yes, they work hard. But they are also articulate speakers. And that, above all else, is the source of their power.

"Speaking well is considered the *number one reason* for career advancement," Virginia Avery asserts in *The Power of Your Speech*. "Every time you meet with a client or make a presentation, your image is affected—for better or worse."

Woodrow Wilson, Avery points out, understood the importance of communicating effectively. He began his career as a reserved political science professor with a stilted speaking style. When he decided to go into politics, he set about becoming a skillful orator. By the time he delivered his inaugural address as the 28th President of the United States, it was said, "Not since Lincoln has there been a president so wonderfully gifted in the art of expression."

Lincoln's prowess as a speaker is beautifully illustrated by a story told by Peggy Noonan in *On Speaking Well*.

"When the famed orator Edward Everett spoke before Lincoln at Gettysburg, he went on for more than two hours and pulled out all the stops with poetry and pleading and stentorian phrases. Then Lincoln got up and offered a masterpiece of compression, two or three minutes on the meaning of war and the meaning of the day. . . . With great grace [Everett] wrote Lincoln, 'I shall be glad if I could flatter myself that I came as near to the central idea of the occasion in two hours as you did in two minutes.'"

Persuasive speaking skills helped most of America's most influential presidents "get their most cherished programs through Congress and leave their stamp on the future," wrote Michael Kazin in the *Washington Post*. Every modern president "who left office with his popularity intact"—from Theodore and Franklin D. Roosevelt to John F. Kennedy to Ronald Reagan—said Kazin, was a masterful speaker.

If skillful speaking can get you to the top of your field, clumsy speaking can get you into trouble.

Consider these common problems that are caused by poor communication:

- Being passed over for a job or a raise you deserve.
- Being rejected by someone who doesn't understand you.
- Being treated as invisible by your boss.
- Being treated with disrespect by your spouse or children.
- Getting into unnecessary verbal conflicts.

There is no question about it, being able to communicate persuasively is an important life skill.

So my question to you is this: What are you doing about it?

What are you doing, right now, to become a more powerful speaker? What books are you reading? What programs are you following? What lessons are you taking?

If speaking well is the single fastest way to succeed in any field, why aren't you learning to be better at it?

No doubt your answer to that is "I don't have enough time." But this is the same argument that Stephen Covey poked holes through in *The Seven Habits of Highly Effective People*. In the rush to get everything done that we are given to do every day, he said, we tend to take care of the urgent tasks first and push off the non-urgent ones. Yet, it is the important-but-not-urgent tasks—like improving your speaking skills—that will make the greatest long-term difference in the quality of your life. So you have to make them a priority.

The key to becoming a more powerful speaker, explains Timothy Koegel in *The Exceptional Presenter*, is practice.

"Everyone I've ever studied who has made himself exceptional— Churchill, Reagan—has worked at it," says Koegel. "Most people don't have any idea what they look and sound like when they're presenting, whether they're sitting at a conference table or talking to a group. . . . Since they don't think of themselves as presenters, they don't realize the impact of these skills. But [speaking well] is the easiest way to fast-track a career."

It is impossible to overestimate the value of speaking well. Whether you are negotiating a lease on a car, presenting an idea at a business meeting, having a conversation with a powerful person you've just been introduced to—what you say and how you say it *matters*.

Although I consider myself a writer first and foremost, my skill at speaking has been responsible for most of my most important accomplishments.

- Saying the right thing got me a 25 percent share in the first information product I created. That stake in the business made me a millionaire in less than two years.
- Speaking well landed me additional partnership deals in the years following that first one. As a result, my share of the business grew to include one-third of a group whose yearly revenues exceeded $135 million.
- Less than two years after I first retired at 39, I talked my way into a high-paid gig with a client that has generated a substantial seven-figure income ever since.

Speaking persuasively continues to help me form partnerships and make alliances that are both pleasurable and profitable. So I'm a big advocate of developing speaking skills. And that's why I recommend it to you.

"If all my talents and powers were to be taken from me by some inscrutable Providence and I had my choice of keeping but one," Daniel Webster once said, "I would unhesitatingly ask to be allowed to keep the power of speaking, for through it I would quickly recover all the rest."

Words are innocent and powerless in themselves, Nathaniel Hawthorne said, but they become immensely powerful in the mouth of someone who knows how to use them to persuade others to follow his lead.

And it doesn't take much. If you improve your speaking skills by just 10 percent, you will double your personal power.

Think of the many times in your daily life that you could benefit from being a persuasive speaker. Think of the conversations you have with your spouse, your children, your colleagues, your boss, and your employees.

Imagine if you could convince anybody of anything.

Imagine how much you could achieve.

Becoming a powerful speaker is not that difficult. Like any skill, it can be acquired if you are willing to put in the time to practice. In this section, I am going to outline three steps to becoming a more powerful speaker. You can take all three of these steps immediately. And you will notice the difference as soon as you start.

Persuasive speaking involves strategic thinking. Inarticulate people suffer not so much from ignorance of how to use language but from the habit of lazy thinking. Lazy thinking results in half-baked notions and contradictory thoughts. And that, in turn, contributes to grammatical, syntactical, and diction mistakes.

Step One: Figure Out What You Want

Let's say you've been invited to take part in a business meeting . . . or perhaps you're gearing up to have an important conversation with a family member. Spend some time beforehand thinking about the topic you will be discussing. Figure out how you can benefit from the meeting. Set a specific, measurable goal for yourself. Then figure out how you can achieve that goal.

This may seem like an unnecessary step. You might be thinking, "I don't need to think about what I want. I am always aware of that. It's not necessary."

In fact, most people don't know what they want. They have some general impressions about being wealthy or successful. But they don't analyze those impressions. They don't break them down. They don't understand how to achieve them strategically.

Step Two: Figure Out What You Can Give Others

Contrary to what some self-improvement gurus will tell you, you won't get what you want in life simply by asking for it. (Possible exception: You look like Brad Pitt or Angelina Jolie.)

Everybody is ultimately motivated by self-interest. Achieving your specific goal, therefore, is a matter of figuring out how you can satisfy the desires of others.

If, for example, your goal for that business meeting you've been invited to is to be nominated to head up an upcoming project, plan for it by making a mental list of how your nomination will help each person attending the meeting. Think about what each person wants. Figure out how, in leading the project, you can provide that.

Most important, think about how you can direct the project so that it will achieve growth and profitability for the company. Spend some time formulating the phrases you will use to drive that point home.

By putting the company first, you will enlist the respect and support of just about everyone. You will establish yourself as a natural leader. And then, when you explain how the project will benefit people individually, you will see how quickly they line up to support you.

Step Three: Take Time to Consider the Objections

After figuring out how you can achieve your goal by providing benefits to others, make a list of the objections you might encounter.

Good copywriters do this every time they write a promotional package. Good public speakers do this before presenting a speech. You should do it, too, before making any informal presentation.

Of course, it's not enough to list objections. You must find good responses for them. You must craft concise arguments that will overcome those objections. You must show your listeners that you are sympathetic to their concerns and that you have a plan to deal with them.

Break the objections down into their component parts. Analyze those parts. Discover their weaknesses or find ways to minimize them. Base your thinking on research if you have time to do it. But also think about your past experience. Remember that your ultimate objective is to find a goal that is good not just for you but for the people you're speaking to. If you do that, you will be able to find the solutions you need.

Ready, Fire, Aim

Most of us, most of the time, speak impulsively. We are stimulated by some event or remark and utter the first thing that pops into our heads. We don't stop to consider the effect our statement will have on those to whom we are speaking. And neither do we consider how our words will affect us. Yet they surely do.

"Words are all we have," Samuel Beckett said. When it comes to many aspects of our life, this is often true.

You can't force your colleagues to listen to your ideas. You can't force your boss to give you a raise or a promotion. You can't force your spouse to agree with everything you say. But if you learn how to think strategically, you can speak persuasively when you need to. And that will make a big difference in your life and your career.

THE RIGHT WAY TO TAKE A WORKING VACATION

You wake up at 6:30, refreshed after a good sleep, and look out your hotel window at Kensington Gardens, already lit up with sunlight. Summer days in England, you remember, are very long.

"So much the better," you think, for it's going to be a good day. You throw on sweats and take the elevator down to the small lobby of the Milestone Hotel. The receptionist and concierge wish you a bright "Good morning." Outside in the shade, the air is bracingly cool. But across the street in the park, you are warm in the morning sun. Walking along the pond, you feel glad to be in London.

At 7:00, you are having breakfast in the hotel restaurant. Twenty minutes later, you are in a taxi passing Westminster Abbey on your way to work. "I've got to see that again," you remind yourself. At 7:30, you are sitting at your desk in the temporary office they've set up for you. Your view from the seventh floor of the Sea Containers House overlooks the Thames.

For the next four hours, you help run this business. There are meetings to attend, interviews to conduct, memos to write and read. It is an ordinary working day in some respects, but it's more intense and is finished before noon. At 11:30, you are exercising. Ninety minutes later, you are having lunch in Wagamama's, a trendy Asian restaurant near your hotel.

The afternoon is devoted to fun: sightseeing, shopping, gallery hunting. You return to the hotel at 6:00 for a sauna or a nap, and then dress for dinner at a local restaurant that the concierge has recommended. You enjoy Prosecco with your first course (a yellow bean salad), Bordeaux with your second course (a grass-fed steak), and a Muscat with dessert (berries and cream). Walking home, passing white stone townhouses that you guess must be worth $5 million to $10 million apiece, you enjoy a small Tuscanella cigar.

By 10:00, you are comfortably settled in your bed, a good book in hand, looking forward to another amazing day.

Welcome to the four-hour workday.

What I've just described is more or less the life I lived for about six weeks in the summer of 2008.

The summer before, I had taken my first working vacation. I spent the month of June in Chicago, writing *Ready, Fire, Aim* in the morning and touring the city with K in the afternoon. It worked out great—both in terms of the amount of work I got done and the amount of fun K and I had. So in 2008 I extended my "working vacation" to six weeks.

It was a nice schedule. But I'm not fooling myself. It's not something I could have done years ago, when my business interests needed more of my attention. Nor is it something I can do now all year round. But for six (maybe eight?) weeks a year, yes.

You can do it, too—enjoy a working vacation of half-days. The idea is that instead of taking a two- or three-week vacation without work, take a four- to six-week vacation working just four hours a day.

In 2007, Timothy Ferriss published a book called *The 4-Hour Workweek*. It was on the bestseller lists for months.

The book's success is a tribute to his great skill at social media advertising. (MaryEllen Tribby and I take a look at what he did in Chapter 4 of our 2008 book *Changing the Channel: 12 Easy Ways to Make Millions for Your Business*.) But it is also due to its title: The idea that you can run a profitable business working just four hours a week is very tempting. Who wouldn't want to do that?

In the book, Ferriss says he managed to reduce his workweek to four hours by using freelance executives and services linked together by the Internet. I only half-believe him. I believe he was able to keep his business going by working only a few hours a week while he was traveling to Asia. But when he came back home, I'll bet his working hours shot way up—maybe even into the 60- to 80-hour workweeks that are normal for successful entrepreneurs.

Ferriss admits that spending so little time on his business when he was away created some problems—including customer service problems—that he had to straighten out when he got back. That's not a business practice you want to perpetuate. Good service means good service all the time—which is what you have to provide if you want to develop a multimillion-dollar business.

> *Every man who possibly can should force himself to a holiday of a full month in a year, whether he feels like taking it or not.*
> *—William James*

Timothy Ferriss's four-hour workweek is an exaggeration. But it's a useful exaggeration, because it emphasizes a welcome fact: that you don't have to work 60 to 80 hours a week, 50 weeks a year, to have a good business. You can take extended vacations. And during those vacations, you can work much less than you do when you are home.

But I don't think you can get away with just four hours a week. I'm happy with four hours a day.

I recommend *The 4-Hour Workweek* because it's full of the kind of good sensible advice you can get only from people who have succeeded by doing what they're telling you to do—though I doubt Ferriss has been able to live his dream since the debut of his book. While it's true that you can put your business on remote control when it is small and stagnant—and if you have very good people helping you run it—once it starts growing, the way Ferriss's business must be growing, you can't possibly neglect it benignly. And make no mistake about it, working only four hours a week is benign neglect.

Growing businesses create new and challenging problems for the entrepreneur. These are not the sort of problems that can be delegated to the troops. The founding father must get involved at some level. And if the business is growing quickly, this demand alone will consume more than four hours a week.

If you want to grow your business—and enjoy the benefits of a growing business—don't set your heart to the dream of the four-hour workweek. It's much more realistic to assume you'll be working 60 to 80 hours a week. That's how much time most of the successful business owners and executives I know work.

But once you have hired a few superstars to help you run your business, you can start working on reducing your hours from 80 to 60 and then to 40. And you can start extending your vacations from zero to two weeks to four and to eight, while working four-hour days as I did in 2008.

I like and recommend the four-hour workday extended vacation. I like it better—much better—than a shorter vacation where I'm doing nothing. Extended, half-day working vacations offer the following benefits:

- You don't have to worry about anything really bad happening to your business while you are on vacation.
- For four hours a day, you focus on the most important, most rewarding business work you do.
- You give your superstars a chance to upgrade their skills and build their confidence (which makes it easier for you to take another, possibly longer, extended vacation next year).
- If you are vacationing with a friend or spouse, you give them the chance to do their thing while you are doing yours.
- You never feel guilty about being on vacation.

It helps, of course, to have an international business like I have, with offices in top vacation spots like Paris and London and Buenos Aires. But even if your business is based entirely in the United States, you can still take an extended working vacation somewhere else—in Europe or the Caribbean, for example—as long as the place you choose has high-speed Internet access, which is almost universal today.

Here's all you have to do:

- **Schedule the time.** If you plan to take two weeks of workless vacation, schedule four weeks of half-days.
- **Identify your priorities.** To stay on top of the most important aspects of your business, analyze how you currently spend your time and identify the tasks that have the biggest long-term effect on profitability. Generally speaking, 20 percent of the work you do will create 80 percent of the long-term profits. Figure out what those tasks are. During your vacation, focus on them.
- **Identify your time wasters.** While you are identifying your most productive tasks, identify your biggest time wasters. If you're like me, most of them have to do with e-mail. So, well before you leave, let everyone you work with know that you'll be on vacation— and ask them to e-mail you only if absolutely necessary. (You'll be amazed by how many questions and concerns people can handle on their own if you give them a chance—which you should be doing anyway.)
- **Stick to your schedule.** You'll be tempted to work more than four hours a day as demands for your time come in. Resist it. A vacation that involves six- or eight-hour workdays is unfair to your vacationing partner and not much fun at all. The best way I've found to stick with my schedule is to get to work before everybody else so I have some time alone (which is what I did in London) and schedule something (like my 12:00 jujitsu workout) that forces me to leave on time.

So here's something you can do today . . . something fun over a glass of wine this evening. Get out an atlas or go online . . . take that mental tour of the world . . . and start dreaming. Then decide where you'll be spending your first working vacation.

READ TO SUCCEED

The average American adult reads about 150 words a minute. At that rate, a 500-page book would take 24 hours to finish. If you had two hours a day to devote to it, you could read a book every two weeks.

Twenty-six books a year. That's just a fraction of the great business books that are published—books that can help you work smarter. And when you consider everything else you read—magazines, newspapers, business reports, e-mails, and so forth—it's obvious that you can't gather enough of the information you need by going about it in a conventional way.

To read for success you need two things:

1. A way to select good stuff to read.
2. A way to read that good stuff faster.

How to Select the Good Stuff to Read

Deciding what to read is by far the most important part of this. Your brain is fundamentally a sophisticated computer. If you put good stuff into it, you will get good stuff out of it. If you fill it with junk, your thinking will be junky.

When you read for success, you read with a purpose. You are looking for ideas that can inspire you, strategies that can inform you, and facts and figures that can help you do a better job. But since you will never have time to read 95 percent of what is published in your field, you need to be sure that the 5 percent you can read is the best.

Unfortunately, most of what is out there is useless or banal or both. And as Ralph Waldo Emerson said, "There are many things of which a wise man might wish to be ignorant."

In earlier chapters, I've pointed out that just about every experience in life—including reading—can be categorized as enriching, neutral, or negative. I have labeled these categories golden, vaporous, and acidic.

Some of what you choose to read will be acidic—downright bad for you. Most of it will be vaporous—neither hurting nor helping you. And only a small portion of it will be golden—changing you for the better.

Promise yourself that you will read only gold from now on. Make a deliberate decision to do that by creating a reading list.

Your reading list should include books (both business books and works of fiction), magazines, and newspapers—in print and/or online. And it should have two parts: a must-read-this-year section and a wish list of everything you'd like to read but don't have time for.

The must-read section has to be limited to what you can actually read. The wish list can be almost any length, and is useful as a resource to draw upon at the end of the year when you create the next year's must-read list.

I keep my wish list on my computer. It includes such books as *Harry Potter* and *War and Peace*, such magazines as the *Nation* and *Esquire*, and such newspapers as the *London Times* and *Le Monde*. My must-read-this-year list is much longer. It includes three newspapers, four magazines, 24 e-zines, 52 business books, and 12 works of fiction.

I don't read every issue of every magazine and e-zine on my "must" list. Nor do I read all of those newspapers every day. I have developed a method of rotating through them each week so that I am constantly stimulated with good ideas. And when I read business books, I use a speed-reading technique that I'll explain in a minute.

The point is that having a reading list allows me to make a conscious decision once a year about what I'm going to read. It's not up to impulse. It's not up to someone else. It is based on my own judgment about what will be good for me. I'm looking for the gold. I don't have time to spend on anything else.

How to Read the Good Stuff Faster

When I was a teenager, I was taught how to speed-read. I tripled my reading speed, but soon lost much of that skill because I didn't practice it.

As an adult, I've read a number of books and articles on speed-reading and have developed my own system. Using this method, I have read a 359-page book on marketing in 55 minutes, four weekly magazines in 31 minutes, and the Sunday *New York Times* in 16 minutes (a rate that even my high-school speed-reading teacher couldn't match). More important, I still remember (and use) a million-dollar idea I learned from that book, a time-management technique I got from one of those magazines, and a handful of interesting facts from that issue of the *Times*.

Reading stuff fast, after all, is not what's important. Retaining it . . . and using it . . . that's how you change your life. "The worth of a book is to be measured by what you can carry away from it," as James Bryce once said.

Here is my system for reading business books and magazines:

- **First, skim the table of contents.** This will give you a quick idea of what the book or magazine has to offer.
- **Next, highlight one or several items you want to read.** Don't be greedy. You don't have time to read everything, and it would be foolish to try. Select the content that you think might have the greatest long-term impact on your career.
- **Now review those highlighted items and see if there is a common thread.** What you are looking for is a Useful Big Idea (UBI)—a principle or perspective that is new to you and that can make you smarter, happier, or more successful.

    Your job is to find that UBI, understand it, and figure out how it fits in your life. With that limited objective in mind, you will be able to sprint through the material—ignoring everything that is tangential and/or irrelevant to your purpose.
- **When you find what you are looking for—the UBI— highlight the sections of the book or article that help you understand it.** Continue speed-reading until you have what you need. Then stop.
- **Make it a point to bring up the UBI in a conversation or e-mail communication.** Do that within 24 hours so it sinks in and begins to stimulate you. Do it again within the next 24 hours. And then do it one more time.

Studies show that we forget 80 percent of what we learn within 24 hours, and most of the remaining 20 percent in the week that follows. By focusing your attention on one UBI and referencing it three times in 72 hours, you will find that it will stay with you and eventually find its way into your decision-making process.

Of course, some business books have more than one UBI. A good example would be the book MaryEllen Tribby and I co-wrote,

Changing the Channel: 12 Easy Ways to Make Millions for Your Business. It is a gold mine of ideas. Each of its 12 chapters teaches you how to master one important marketing channel.

To speed-read a book like *Changing the Channel*, you would review the table of contents, looking for two or three chapters that you believed could have an immediate impact on your career. (*Immediate* is the key word here. You don't want to spend your valuable time learning skills you can't implement right away.) Of those two or three, you would select one and look for its UBI.

You might, for example, decide that you wanted to learn about telemarketing, e-mail marketing, and print advertising . . . in that order. So you would start by reading the chapter on telemarketing, looking for its UBI, and highlighting the paragraphs that best explained it to you. Then you would use what you learned in conversations over a three-day period. By that time, what you had learned would have sunk in. Then you would go on to the chapter on e-mail marketing and the next UBI.

This method works. I've been using it for just over a year, and I'm much better at applying the stuff I read than I was before. Phrases come to mind. Terminology. Titles and authors.

It makes my thinking more "linked." I am starting to see how certain popular business and financial ideas correspond to ideas about art and literature. It also makes me speak more confidently. And I believe it makes my arguments more credible.

I'm convinced that this is the smart way to gather information:

1. **Read less, learn more.** Don't feel you have to take in the entire content. Search for useful big ideas. Focus on one UBI at a time. Get it. Repeat it. Put it to work.
2. **Learn to scan.** When reading books, give prefaces and/or first chapters your greatest attention, because they are likely to contain most of the useful big ideas. Then read the first paragraph of the rest of the chapters and the first sentence of each paragraph below the first one. This technique will help you locate the big ideas fast.
3. **Make it fun.** The purpose of learning is not necessarily to have a good time, but if you care about what you are doing, and do it seriously, it will be fun.

Read less. Read better. Read faster. Have fun and learn.

Part Seven

THE OBSTACLES TO YOUR SUCCESS— AND HOW TO DEFEAT THEM

WHEN DISASTER STRIKES

Your doctor reads your EKG and says, "Holy cow! I've never seen anything like this before!"

You walk out to your car in the morning—and find all four wheels gone.

You left your bag, with all your IDs and banking information, on the subway.

Sometimes life dishes out these little disasters. How you react to them says much about your character and bears heavily on your ability to carry out a successful life.

The first time I lost my wallet, my first thought was doomsday: A highly skilled theft ring had taken it and already emptied all my bank accounts. That tells you I am prone to panic. K will attest to that.

She has had to remind me on countless occasions not to panic, that "chances are everything will turn out fine."

Having a positive disposition is very helpful when you are faced with a challenge—big or small. But I've learned that even bleak-minded people like yours truly can overcome their fears and respond to a crisis positively by following a few simple guidelines.

My nephew is a lot like his uncle. Recently, he got himself into a bind at the college he goes to. He acted imprudently and broke a few rules. Now he's facing disciplinary action. What had begun as a very promising college career at a great university has metamorphosed into a potential disaster.

He's worried, he told me—so worried that he can't think straight. He's imagining Armageddon. Sleeping fitfully. Distracted at work.

I know how he feels. I'd feel the same way if I were in his situation. But I've had enough experience by now to know that you can't give in to your fears. When you are faced with a threatening challenge, it's difficult to push ahead. But if you don't find a way to do so, your productivity can quickly shrink to zero, and your life can be put on permanent hold.

You don't want that to happen. So the next time disaster strikes you, follow the protocol I suggested to my nephew:

1. Make Friends with Your Fear

What is it that is scaring you? It is probably some "worst-case" scenario that you keep running through your mind.

Some people will remind you that most of the time worst-case scenarios don't unfold. That's why they call them worst-case. "Don't worry about that," they'll tell you. "It probably won't happen, so get it out of your head."

But such advice is useless to the person who has already got the worst-case scenario in his head. It is, after all, a very scary movie. And he's the star of it. Not thinking about it is not an option.

The solution that works for me is to let the movie play itself out in its entirety. I allow myself to imagine the worst, vividly and in detail. And then I find some way to see myself living satisfactorily with that dire reality.

If, for example, I am imagining identity thieves stealing all my assets and leaving me in penury, I imagine myself being happy to go back to work and start over again. I run a mental movie of myself waking up the next day and starting a new business on the change that is in my pocket, and gradually rebuilding my wealth and a successful career.

By letting the bad movie play out and giving it a happy ending, you can exorcise the fear and return to an emotionally positive state. Only by finding a way to "accept" the worst can you find the peace to take positive action.

Chances are things will not turn out as you have imagined, but if they do, you are emotionally prepared for them. You won't panic. You won't cry. You will move forward according to your plan.

2. Look for the Silver Lining

Every disaster has a silver lining. Even terminal cancer does. You have some amount of time to organize the end of your life and say your goodbyes. You wouldn't have that chance if your fate were to get run over by a train.

Identify what is good about a bad situation and spend some time thinking about that. If you do it sincerely and repeatedly, it will bring you some emotional comfort.

Eventually—if you are very successful at doing this—you may even find yourself feeling grateful for the problem.

3. Develop a Plan

You need a plan to deal with the problem. The plan should be multi-leveled, since you can't know how the situation will play out.

A good disaster plan should deal with at least three eventualities: worst case, bad case, good case. Articulate each one clearly and in detail. Then find solutions to, or at least responses for, each of those details.

4. Take Action

Making friends with your fear, finding a silver lining, and developing an action plan will make you feel 100 percent better—and you can do all that in a matter of hours, days at the most. But that improvement in your emotional state won't last unless you start acting on your plan.

Action—as in all other areas of life—is critical when you are faced with disaster. The moment you start moving your response plan forward, you'll be making progress and lessening the chances that things will end up badly.

You'll feel better about yourself the moment you start, and will continue to feel better so long as you are taking positive action.

GIVING UP YOUR INFORMATION ADDICTION

I hadn't seen Dave in almost 20 years. He was my dentist when we moved to Boca Raton in the early 1980s. He continued to take care of K and the kids after we moved to Delray Beach 10 years later, but I opted for dental care closer to home.

Dave contacted me when he discovered that I was the man behind the "Michael Masterson" pen name. He'd been receiving *Early to Rise* for a while and liking it. One day, he went to the web site and saw my photo. "I know that guy!" he thought. So he got my e-mail address from K. "How about lunch?" he wrote. "I've got a bunch of things I need to ask you."

Several weeks later, we were eating chopped chicken salads at City Oyster on Atlantic Avenue. Dave seemed nervous. It was as if he were intimidated by the Michael Masterson persona. I did my best to assure him I was the same person who used to wince in pain when he cleaned my teeth. We talked a bit about family news, but it was clear he had something else on his mind.

On his mind was a decision he was trying to make: Should he spend $100,000 on the highest level of an Internet-marketing program he had been looking at?

"I've been studying their stuff," he told me. "It's really good. But I'm not sure it makes sense for me to invest that kind of money."

"A hundred grand is a lot of money," I said. I felt like Sam Spade talking to Gutman about the price of the Maltese Falcon.

"But you get an awful lot for your money," Dave explained. "They do all the technical stuff for you, which I'm not very good at. All I'd have to do is come up with the ideas."

"Well," I said, practicing my best Sam Spade drawl, "what ideas do you have?"

In fact, Dave didn't have a single one. "All I know is that I am in the wrong business," he said. "I took this self-test online—and I found out I'm in the worst business in the world for me."

At nearly 50 years of age, Dave had just concluded that his entire career had been a waste. "I wanted to be a dentist since I was eight years old," he told me. "If I had known then what a bad business it was for me, I would have done something else."

"Like what?" I asked.

"Like what you do," he said. He was smiling, but he looked serious.

"Look," I told him. "My business is a great business—but I don't think you should conclude that your life has been wasted simply because you took some pop quiz that was probably designed to sell you something."

"But it was right," he insisted. "It proved something I had always known but was afraid to admit."

The waitress filled our drinks. We ate in silence for a while.

"So what I'm thinking is that, since I'm not into the technical stuff, this Internet-marketing program would be very good for me."

"How much time have you invested in learning about Internet marketing?" I asked.

"About three years," he answered.

"And how many information products on the subject have you bought in that three-year period?" I asked.

Dave laughed. "I can't even count that high," he said.

"How much money have you spent?"

"Tens of thousands. Probably more."

"And yet, you haven't actually started an Internet-marketing business," I said.

He nodded, then rattled off the names of every Internet-marketing program he'd bought—all the ones that I knew and dozens of others I had never heard of.

"That's a lot of buying," I told him.

"Tell me about it," he said.

Information is not knowledge.

—*Albert Einstein*

Dave explained that when he reads an advertising promotion pitching a new Internet-marketing product, he is "totally taken in by it," even though he realizes he is just reading "a sales pitch."

"But even though I know that I'm being seduced by a professional wordsmith, I can't stop myself from buying."

"I hear you," I said. "You are an information junkie."

"You think?"

"I do."

"What about you?" he said. "I read that you read a lot of informational books—about one every week."

"I do," I said, "but I'm not an information junkie. I'm an information user."

"So what's the difference?"

I explained that the difference is huge. An information junkie is addicted to the process of buying information. Although he may delude himself into thinking otherwise, he has no intention of ever using the information he buys. An information user is very practical about his purchases. He buys information for specific, pragmatic purposes. He uses the information he buys to achieve specific goals—to start or grow a business, to learn a new language, to improve his negotiating skills.

An information junkie is happiest at the moment he is buying the information. His enthusiasm soon wanes, however. Within hours or days of receiving it, the information junkie is on to other things. The new product goes up on the shelf with the old products. He's excited about the next new one.

An information user makes progress. See him reading a book about nutrition, and there's a very good chance (if he likes the book) that his eating habits will change in the immediate future. The information junkie, in contrast, may have 26 books about nutrition in his living room. He may have even read them all—while he was lying on the couch eating potato chips.

An information user is someone who consumes information to profit from it. If he invests $100 in learning about some subject, he expects to see a substantial return on that investment—perhaps a thousand dollars' worth of value, material or spiritual. An information junkie consumes information like drugs or candy bars. It gives him an immediate rush and then nothing afterward. That's why he needs to buy more.

The information user has long-term expectations when it comes to knowledge. He believes the knowledge he acquires now will compound over time as he learns more and is in a better position to leverage what he has learned for greater benefit. The information junkie is in it for the here-and-now. He doesn't believe in saving. He's always on to the next hot thing.

What about you? Are you an information junkie? Take this test and see:

1. In the past year, I've purchased more than 12 books that I haven't read. (If your answer is Yes, give yourself 2 points.)
2. In the past year, I've purchased:
   - Only information products that I have used. (Yes = 1 point)
   - Between one and three $100 information products that I haven't used. (Yes = 2 points)
   - Between three and five $100 information products that I haven't used. (Yes = 3 points)
   - More than five $100 information products that I haven't used. (Yes = 5 points)
3. In the past year, I've purchased at least one $1,000 information product that I didn't use. (Yes = 5 points)
4. I am most excited about the information that I buy:
   - When I am ordering it. (Yes = 3 points)
   - When I receive it. (Yes = 2 points)
   - When I begin using it. (Yes = 1 point)
5. When I read a book, I feel compelled to read it from cover to cover. (Yes = 2 points)
6. I generally take notes when I read something. (Yes = 1 point, No = 2 points)

Well . . . how did you score?

If you scored 8 or above, you are indeed an information junkie. You might think the good people at ETR would like that (since they are in the business of selling information). But they don't. The people at ETR know that their business will grow most strongly if they develop a customer base of information *users* rather than *junkies*. That's because information users benefit from the knowledge they buy. This means they are more discriminating (which favors ETR's products, since they are some of the best in the business), they buy more products in the long run, and they request fewer refunds.

If you are an information junkie, don't despair. You can convert yourself into an information user simply by following two rules:

1. When you buy an information product, set specific deadlines for reading it and implementing what you learn. For instance, set a goal that you will take one of its recommended actions within 24 hours of receiving the product. Then resolve to take at least one more recommended action each week thereafter.
2. Don't buy another product until you have made some progress with the one you previously purchased.

That's all there is to it. Obey these two rules and you'll not only break your addiction, you will radically improve your life.

INFORMATION OVERLOAD: HOW TO ESCAPE THE CRUSH

Stan Connors has a problem. As a regular reader of *Early to Rise*, he's getting so much good stuff from us (he's especially interested in learning how to "eliminate some debt" and retire one day) that he "can't figure out what to read."

"Don't get me wrong," he says. "I love *Early to Rise* and look forward to reading it. But it's too much information all at once."

"What should I do?" he asks.

What should any of us do?

We live in a world that is absolutely flooded with information. Consider these facts:

- The average person receives 32 e-mail messages per day.
- There is enough scientific information written every day to fill seven complete sets of the *Encyclopedia Britannica*.
- The world's production of print, film, optical, and magnetic content in just one year would require roughly 5 exabytes (5 trillion megabytes) of storage, about 800 megabytes per person.

So if you—like Stan Connors—are feeling overwhelmed by information, you're not alone. Information overload is a serious problem for just about everyone.

"One of the most anxiety-inducing side effects of the information era," Richard Saul Wurman says in *Information Anxiety*, "is the feeling that you have to know it all." That is especially true for smart, ambitious people—people who want to improve their lives and realize that getting the right information is a big part of success.

Since you're reading this book, that probably means you.

When you begin a new project or become interested in a new idea, do you have an insatiable desire to learn more about it? Do you find yourself buying—and reading—every book, report, newsletter, and magazine you can find on the subject? (That's what I do.)

In the beginning, it feels great. You are riding high. Then, all of a sudden, you realize that you've become an information junkie. You've been spending so much time reading about whatever it is you want to do that you don't have any time left to actually do it. You feel like crying for help.

Bob Bly calls this "analysis paralysis."

"All the information you are taking in has overloaded your circuits," he says. "You can't process it all, sort through it, and figure out what to do first. So, instead, you do nothing. You take no action—other than to order yet another course or report to read."

Does any of this sound familiar?

Bob has a formula for preventing analysis paralysis. He calls it the 25-25-50 rule. It is based on the fact that there are only three ways to learn a process (e.g., how to start an Internet business) or a skill (e.g., copywriting): studying, observing, and doing.

The 25-25-50 rule says that you must divide your time as follows:

- No more than 25 percent of your time *studying*—i.e., reading books, attending workshops, listening to instructional CDs in your car.
- No more than 25 percent of your time *observing*—watching what successful people are already doing.
- At least 50 percent of your time actually *doing* the thing you are studying and observing.

For example, if you want to sell information products on the Internet, you would spend 25 percent of your time studying material on the way it's done, 25 percent of your time observing the way other people are doing it, and 50 percent of your time creating your first product . . . designing your web site . . . and building your list.

I like Bob's rule because it emphasizes action. And when I found out about it, I wondered if it could be applied to my daily working life. In thinking about it, I concluded that it depended greatly on what sort of work I was doing. If I were learning a new skill, Bob's rule seemed to apply. But when I was going about my normal workday activities—creating new products and growing businesses—my time was spent very differently.

My daily working life, I realized, has three common components:

1. Gathering information.
2. Analyzing that information and using it to make plans.
3. Taking action.

I tend to do my information gathering at specific times. I read newspapers in the early morning, magazines during breaks, and e-mail at the end of the day. I read to encounter useful ideas. I analyze those ideas both as I'm reading them and later on, at odd moments throughout the day. I spend most of my workday—about 80 percent of it—taking action. The rest of my time—20 percent—is devoted to gathering information, analyzing it, and making plans.

I like that 80 percent number. It corresponds with Pareto's Law—the 80/20 rule that you can apply to just about everything.

INFORMATION OVERLOAD: THE E-MAIL PROBLEM

Chris Schroeder—CEO of Health Central Network—bragged at a recent information-publishers' conference that there were 2,000 items in his RSS feed in-box awaiting his attention. When I read this in an article by Bob Bly, I couldn't help but shake my head.

"I have news for Mr. Schroeder," Bob wrote. "If you have 2,000 unread items in your RSS feed, it is anything BUT an ideal way of getting information. Over-subscribing to free content via RSS feeds is an invitation to information overload disaster—equivalent to getting a Sunday *New York Times* delivered to your door every day of the year."

Bob is dead right.

E-mail information overload, in particular, is a huge problem for entrepreneurs and small-business owners. Unfortunately, most of us are more or less addicted to it. Consider these facts, according to an eROI survey:

- 66 percent of Americans read e-mail seven days a week.
- 61 percent continue to check e-mail while on vacation.
- 41 percent check e-mail first thing in the morning.
- 26 percent say they can't go more than two to three days without checking e-mail.

Is that bad?

I believe it is. For one thing, it is a significant cause of stress. In *Bit Literacy: Productivity in the Age of Information and Email Overload*, Mark Hurst says, "It may sound enticing to subscribe to the latest e-newsletter, but it's demoralizing to see a pile of issues awaiting reading. . . ."

But stress is just one problem. Consider this: A psychiatrist at London's King's College administered IQ tests to three groups. Group 1 did nothing but perform the IQ test. Group 2 was distracted by e-mail and ringing phones. Group 3 was stoned on marijuana. Unsurprisingly, Group 1 did better—by an average of 10 points—than the other groups. The e-mailers, however, did—on average—six points worse than the stoners.

As Gertrude Stein pointed out long before e-mail was invented, "Everybody gets so much information all day long that they lose their common sense."

If you want to work smart and happily (and who doesn't?), you need to get control over your e-mail in-box.

The first step, says author Timothy Ferriss, is not to feel guilty. "Recognize that you receive too much information. It's not your fault. Just accept that there is more information than time, and that it's increasing every day."

Ferriss says that there are three ways to deal with e-mail overload. You can "live by reaction" and feel increasingly stressed and confused. You can opt out by not reading anything. Or you can practice "bit literacy" by getting "*some* information—the *right* information—without trying to get all of it."

He recommends going on a "media diet"—that is, getting rid of most of what is coming into your e-mail box and keeping only that which provides useful information on a reliable basis.

You can then divide the good stuff into "worth scanning" and "solid gold." E-mails worth scanning are from sources that reliably deliver at least some relevant information. Solid-gold e-mails are from those rare sources that provide useful tips and insights every single time.

Your solid-gold e-mails should be read first. And both your solid-gold and worth-scanning e-mails should be read not thoroughly but intelligently and strategically—the same way as I've suggested business books should be read.

But even after whittling your in-box down to these two categories and reading the information strategically, you may find that you are still spending too much time on e-mail.

If that is the case, follow the "Power of One" rule. Scan your solid-gold e-mails until you find one good and useful idea—an idea you can implement immediately. Then stop reading.

Remember, you don't have to know everything—or even most of what there is to know—to succeed at most endeavors. There are hundreds of ways to make money on the Internet, for example, but you can easily make a six-figure income by using only a few of them.

And finally, as I've already recommended—you should open your e-mail only once a day, toward the end of the day.

I have repeatedly found that if I read my e-mails first thing in the morning, as so many people do, I'm emotionally exhausted by the time I finish. It saps my energy when I need it most. And then, lacking energy, I don't want to do anything very difficult or important. So I find myself taking care of "cleanup" or "preparation" tasks—the kind that make you feel organized but don't advance your career or help you achieve any of your major objectives.

I have also found that when I try to deal with work-related e-mail in the morning, I spend about twice as much time on it as I should. That's because I tend to get involved in "discussions" that are unimportant or irrelevant to my goals.

As I've said, this type of e-mail is full of the problems that other people are trying to get you to solve for them. If you ignore it until the end of the day, you will find that much of it already will have been taken care of—leaving more time for you to take advantage of the really good stuff, the information-packed, solid-gold e-mails that you really want and need.

HOW TO GET OUT OF THAT DAMNED RUT

Good friend and business partner Leonard asked these questions:

> How do you get out of a rut? Regain passion for your work? Get yourself up for each day? Have you thought about this? It happens to me often. I find it makes me miserable. I feel guilty and useless, because I tend to waste away the day. The only way I get back into it is to get on a good roll with a new project. But sometimes that takes too much time to happen.

What can you say about this experience Leonard describes? That it stinks?

You wake up tired and unmotivated. You dread work. Everything seems more interesting than what you have to do.

The feeling can pass in a few hours, or it can last for days—even weeks. It is entirely unproductive—and completely unnecessary.

I'll tell you how to banish this experience from your life in a moment. But before I do, let's talk about why you occasionally feel this way.

The Following Three Paragraphs May Be Unsuitable for Children and True Believers

The reason you occasionally feel that your work has no meaning is because it has none.

The same goes for your life. The universe is—sorry to say—a void, not a magical kingdom created for your personal amusement.

Meaning—and the passion that goes with it—is not something that exists outside of you. It comes from within you. You can't capture it. You can only create it. The moment you stop creating it, it is gone.

The feeling of malaise you get when you fall into a rut is a letdown of energy—energy that you have been creating all along.

Okay . . . maybe you don't buy that. A meaningless universe might contradict your beliefs. But it doesn't matter. Because what I'm about to tell you will work regardless of whether you understand the cause and effect of it all.

Let me start by giving you two good reasons to feel bad:

1. You have a biochemical imbalance. (If you feel bad a whole lot, get some help.)
2. You are doing something/someone/somewhere wrong.

You Should Be Doing What You Want to Do . . . with Whom You Want to Do It . . . Where You Want to Do It

If you are doing something you really don't like, it might pay to change careers. The same holds true for the key people in your life. If you have surrounded yourself with energy-sucking losers, give them the heave-ho. Same holds true for your neighborhood. Does it really stink? Does it depress you every time you think about it? Do you dream of warm weather and sunny skies? (Come to Florida!)

On the other hand, if you basically like your work/colleagues/location, don't waste any time fantasizing about changing them.

Three Stages to Getting Yourself out of a Rut

I said there is no reason to ever be in a slump. It's true. And here's better news: Getting yourself out of a funk is relatively easy to do.

1. Recognize that you are very low in energy . . . and energy is what you need. Imagine that inside your brain there is a motivation panel. The panel contains dozens of fuses, each one a conductor of energy. When you hit a slump, many of these fuses have blown.

   Blown fuses—any sort of negative, self-deprecating, or self-limiting thoughts—must be removed before they can be replaced with good ones.

   To take out your blown fuses:

   Recognize that your slump will pass. (It passed before, didn't it?)

   Try not to be mad at yourself. (After all, this is basically a biochemical problem.)

   Remind yourself how lucky you are. (There are millions of people worse off.)

If you are worried about a particular problem, imagine the worst outcome and then figure out how you will survive it. This will neutralize the anxiety.

2. Do something—anything—that gives you a little charge. The idea is to think/say/do a number of things that you've found through experience charge you up a little. Some things that work for me might work for you. Try these:

   - Put on some music. Loud. Choose something that will "pump you up," as they say. This morning's selection for me was "Help Me Rhonda" by the Beach Boys. Very therapeutic.
   - Dance. (Make sure no one is looking.)
   - If you can't force yourself to dance, do some kind of wild exercises. Frantic jumping jacks. Leapfrogging across the carpet. (Do this in private, too.)
   - Stand in front of a mirror and smile. Smile 100 times. Did you know that the physical act of smiling releases endorphins? You won't believe it until you try it. Go ahead.

   If you do enough of this stuff . . . and you've really rid yourself of your blown fuses . . . you are ready for the third step (which is really the key to the entire process).

3. Complete a worthwhile task—something useful that has value to you.

   The trick is to have a ready inventory of meaningful tasks that need doing. If you are a busy person, this won't be a problem. The tasks you have set aside in inventory should be relatively small in scope—you should be able to complete them in a few hours at most.

   I can't even begin to guess what your inventory would look like. Mine would most likely include writing something (like a short story, a scene for a screenplay, or a message for *Early to Rise*). It might also include something more mundane (like replacing that light bulb that has been out for six months).

Remember that the job must be important—to you—and you must do it well. If it is and you do, you will be out of your slump by the time you are finished with it.

It works every time. Getting out of a slump is all about forgetting the problems that are draining your energy and getting involved in good, energizing work. The secret is to climb out of the rut in stages. Otherwise, you won't succeed.

One more thing: When you feel a slump coming on, don't ignore it. Act immediately.

You Wouldn't Allow Yourself to Get a Migraine. Why Let Yourself Fall into Despair?

Slumps are like bad headaches. They are terrible, but they usually come on slowly. If you attack them in the beginning, when they are just getting started, you can defeat them. If you wait too long, you are going to suffer.

So the moment you feel moody or depressed or simply listless and unmotivated, recognize those feelings as symptoms of an upcoming illness—and start the three-part cure I've just outlined.

WHEN YOUR LIFE SUDDENLY TAKES A TURN FOR THE WORSE

A new client who agreed to sign up with you suddenly cancels.

A promised promotion evaporates.

The deadline your plumber swore to passes without anything having been done.

The trick to dealing with disappointments like these is to have a "What if it doesn't happen?" plan in place almost from the start.

The idea is to create a Plan B every time you create a Plan A. And if you create a good Plan B and spend some time visualizing it (after you have visualized Plan A), you won't feel disappointed if Plan A falls through.

If, for example, you are hoping to be in London for Christmas this year, go ahead and book the arrangements—but spend a few minutes thinking about what you could do instead if, for whatever reason, the trip falls through. (A special Christmas at home—celebrated in some new and interesting way—may turn out to be even better.)

A fallback plan also works in the event of an unforeseen interruption in your routine. Always being prepared with a list of tasks you have wanted to accomplish for a long time is a good way to turn unexpected downtime into a rich, rewarding experience.

A few years ago, for example, I tore up my knee and had to have surgery that put me on my back for two weeks and off the jujitsu mats for six months. For someone with my schedule (and addictive mentality), this could have been very bad. But since I'd had prior knee injuries and, therefore, knew that I was likely to undergo this operation some day, I had developed a fallback plan that made the recovery time bearable.

My fallback plan for the two weeks in bed (and on painkillers—which meant I couldn't do any meaningful work) was to catch up on all the great movies I had never seen or seen only once. My fallback plan for the six months of jujitsu inactivity was to use the time to rest and restore my shoulders and back, which were seriously ailing.

The movie-watching plan went very well. I saw two or three great movies a day—more than 30 in all. I also managed, during the second week, to read a half-dozen business publications that had accumulated on the corner of my desk. Far from feeling blue and abused, I was in a very good mood during that early period of convalescence—and that was entirely due to the fact that I felt like I was finally getting to things I had long wanted to do.

My fallback plan for the six months of inactivity was more challenging. I still went into the jujitsu academy every free moment (and I occasionally helped out with a lesson), but, mostly, I was frustrated by not being able to train again—a feeling that intensified as my knee got better.

But because I used that time to have my shoulders and back worked on, after putting it off for more than three years, I felt that I was accomplishing something. And because of all the care I took in healing my body, when I finally began training again, I was able to compete for the first time in years with an injury-free (though age-addled) body. That felt good.

Spend five minutes today asking yourself:

- "What positive development in my career am I counting on right now?"
- "What will I do if it doesn't happen?"

Then ask yourself the same questions about your personal life.

If you don't have a fallback plan, develop one. When you do, make sure it's something you can be happy with. If it isn't, work on it some more. You'll find that the more time you spend refining it, the more attractive it will become.

And in case you unexpectedly end up with time on your hands, prepare now by making a list of projects and/or tasks that you have always wanted to do. (Have you been thinking about writing a novel? Researching your family tree? Have you long been frustrated because you can't speak a foreign language? Can't dance the salsa?)

Spend some casual time thinking about your "dream" projects, refining them, and imagining how you can make them happen. The more time you spend doing this, the more excited you'll be about it. And then, when the time comes (and it almost certainly will), you will move from disappointment to anticipation in no time flat.

NINE STEPS TO DEFEATING DEPRESSION

Of all the many prescriptions for happiness that populate the media these days, the most popular one is also the least helpful. I'm talking about the idea that you can defeat depression by "paying attention to yourself."

The truth is that paying attention to yourself doesn't make you happy at all. In fact, the *more* attention you give yourself, the *less* happy you are likely to be. Focusing inward can perpetuate your feelings of hopelessness.

60 Minutes correspondent Mike Wallace defined depression this way: "Sunshine means nothing to you. The seasons, friends, or good food mean nothing. All you do is focus on yourself and how badly you feel."

Think of the least-happy people you know. What are they always talking about? Their accomplishments. Their troubles. Their hopes. Their worries. Their this. Their that. In short, *themselves*.

I have a friend. Let's call her Shelly. Shelly is a smart, good-looking woman, but she can't maintain long-term relationships. She has no idea why this is true. "People are always disappointing me," she says. And she has stories.

We have lunch together two or three times a year. And at every meeting, Shelly talks non-stop about all the people who have failed her. She complains about her boss. She bitches about her husband. She does it with a certain sense of humor—but it is all "Wah! Wah! Wah! What about me?"

I've suggested to Shelly that she would be happier if she did some volunteer work or took on a hobby. Perhaps get a pet. But she doesn't listen.

To the outside observer, Shelly has nothing to complain about. She has perfect health. She has a healthy family. And she is financially independent—putting her among the luckiest people on earth. Yet from her perspective—from the inside—she sees nothing but negatives.

You probably have a Shelly in your life. Maybe more than one.

The trouble with the Shellys of the world is that they spend too much of their valuable time thinking and talking about themselves. Their lives never get any better. And they can't figure out why. They believe the solution lies in getting other people to feel sorry for them. They don't understand that seeking attention is a big part of their problem.

I have a theory about why this is so.

There are essentially two impulses in the universe: contraction and relaxation. Everything—every animate and inanimate thing—is, literally, becoming more or less dense at any given moment. The ultimate denseness is a black hole, which sucks in light but gives out none.

As psychological creatures, our consciousness is always in flux between the contraction and the dissolution of the ego. Our egocentric impulses are the source of much of the work we do and the art we create, but they are also the source of tension, sickness, and despair. Our dissolution impulses are the source of our loving relationships. They relax us and prepare us to accept the ultimate dissolution of the ego, which is death.

Contraction gives us the egoistic pleasure of being loved—being acknowledged and appreciated. Relaxation gives us the exocentric pleasure of doing the loving—of our work, our lives, and the people who inhabit them.

Both contraction and relaxation can deliver pleasure, but the pleasure of contraction (the pleasure of the ego) is temporary, whereas the pleasure of relaxation is the enduring pleasure of the soul.

It feels good to have people pay attention to you. But even at its most intense (imagine being a movie star), the pleasure dissipates almost as soon as the attention shifts away. And when the pleasure of the ego leaves, a vacuum of sadness takes its place.

It's like taking drugs. The effect is temporary. It's addictive. It leaves you wanting more. And each time you get more, it is not enough. Eventually, it kills you.

"Enough of all this deep thinking," you say. "What does this have to do with me?"

Just this: The next time you are feeling sad or angry, recognize that there is a way to become happy again. Relax your ego.

Here's how:

1. **Accept the fact that it is perfectly normal to feel crummy *sometimes*.** Despite your core strengths and your many accomplishments, you will occasionally find yourself down in the dumps. It's natural for ambitious people to feel that way. As productivity expert Timothy Ferriss says, "The occasional bouts of self-doubt and sadness are an integral part of building anything remarkable."

2. **If you are upset because of something you did to yourself, forgive yourself.** It's okay. You screwed up. What matters is what you do next, not what you just did.

   I sometimes get angry when I feel pressured by work obligations. But when I examine the reason for all the work, it's usually because I volunteered to take it on in the first place. When I recognize that my mood is being affected by my own prior actions, I remind myself that I'm lucky. "It's okay that you are angry. But you don't have to be. You can get through today. And you can have better discipline tomorrow." That's what I tell myself, and it helps me feel better instantly.

3. **If you are upset because of something someone else did to you, take a chill pill.** Count to 10. Recognize that you can't control the behavior of other people. The only thing you can control is your *response* to their behavior. Nobody can take that away from you.

   "Between stimulus and response there is a space," said Viktor Frankl, author of *Man's Search for Meaning*. "In that space is our power to choose our response. In our response lies our growth and our freedom."

I used to get upset when my family, friends, or colleagues made a mistake. I realize now how stupid that was. It didn't do me any good. And it made me unproductive, unhappy, and unpleasant to be around. I changed by learning to **turn the other cheek**. The moment I stopped resenting others for their shortcomings, I began to feel better about myself.

It's amazing how well this works.

Somebody bumps into you on the street, and you sprain your ankle. You have a choice. You can be angry at that person. You can be upset with yourself for not being more aware of your surroundings. Or you can forgive the person and yourself and change the way you think about your injury. Rather than rue the inconvenience of being laid up for a week or two, see the recuperation period as a gift—the chance to start a new project or catch up on your reading.

4. **Don't allow unrealistic expectations to interfere with your relationships. (This is a subcategory of not allowing the behavior of other people to upset you.)** Instead of being upset by your spouse's habit of (fill in the blank), resolve to accept the fact that she won't be changing and find a way to forgive her and even love her for her frailty. Instead of being angry that your child is a slob, find a way to love him for his strengths while gently teaching him (by showing, not telling) the advantages of being orderly. Instead of being angry at your business partner because she didn't perform as well as you expected her to, learn to appreciate what she brings to the table and negotiate a new deal with her without anger.

    Accepting people for who they are does not mean allowing them to make your life miserable. On the contrary, it means being realistic—realizing that 90 percent of the time a person's fundamental characteristics cannot be changed. If you find a certain behavior unacceptable, you change the way you deal with it (something you can do) instead of trying to change the person (which you can't do).

5. **If you are upset because of circumstances beyond your control, take a double dose of chill pill.** As Alex

Green, Investment Director of the Oxford Club and Chairman of Investment U, said in his article *The Psychology of Optimal Experience*, you can deal with your troubles more effectively if you define them as "problems" (which can be solved) or "predicaments" (which can be coped with).

Getting caught in a storm or catching a cold is not a reason to get mad at yourself. Neither, by the way, is being caught in a worldwide economic collapse.

6. **If you are unhappy at work, find a way to care about what you're doing.** As Albert Camus said, "But what is happiness except the simple harmony between a man and the life he leads?" You won't experience happiness if you work at a job you hate or if you do poor work on a project you like. But if you learn to care about the work you do, you will find that your energy will improve, and you will start to enjoy it.

7. **Engage in some sport or challenging exercise—something that is so demanding you can't do it while thinking.** Walking, stretching, and yoga are great forms of exercise. If you do them with a tranquil mind, they will make you healthy and happy, too. But if you do them when you are sad and feeling sorry for yourself, they will give you no relief. You will forget about the exercise and focus on your negative thoughts. That will make things worse.

8. **Recognize that the health of your body has a great deal to do with your mood. If you are feeling bad much of the time, you probably need to make a few lifestyle changes. To wit:**
   - **Eat healthfully.** Eating too many carbohydrates will make you crazy, cranky, and tired. To have consistent energy all day, use food like fuel. Eat six smallish meals a day, avoiding junk food and favoring organics, lean meats, and plenty of protein.
   - **Sleep and rest adequately.** For me, adequate sleep is a major contributor to feeling good. Studies show that people who get seven good hours of sleep a night live longer, suffer from fewer illnesses, and achieve more because they have more energy. If you get tired during the day, take a short nap.
   - **Get the advice of a good doctor about antidepressants.** I'm generally against putting chemicals in my body.

I much prefer natural cures. But antidepressants have helped some people close to me and may help you, too.

9. **Take positive steps to focus "outward" instead of "inward"—to pay less attention to yourself and more attention to others.** A few examples:

- Make your friends happy. Smile when you see them. Listen to their stories. Give them the advice they want and shut up when they don't want any. Become the person they turn to when the chips are down. Learn to love their peccadilloes and encourage them to overcome their faults. Above all, be loyal.

- Be a reliable and steady resource for your business colleagues. Help them achieve their goals—not because you want them to reciprocate in some way but simply because you care about them and want them to succeed.

- Do something for someone you don't know—a stranger you come upon, a foster child, or a sick or poor person who can benefit from your help. Spend time and money.

Make this outward focus a natural part of your daily life. Do it purposefully and deliberately until it becomes second nature. You will know when that happens, because you'll be feeling happy most of the time—and when you become sad or angry, you'll be able to get over it quickly and easily.

Part Eight

BUILDING YOUR WEALTH

HOW MUCH ARE YOU WORTH? FIGURE IT OUT AND MAKE YOUR LIFE MUCH, MUCH RICHER

A French woman, upon seeing Picasso in a Parisian restaurant, approached the great master and insisted that he put down his coffee and make a quick sketch of her. Graciously, Picasso obliged. When he was done, she took the drawing, put it in her handbag, and then pulled out her billfold.

"How much do I owe you?" she asked.

"$5,000," was Picasso's reply.

"$5,000? But it took you only three minutes!" she exclaimed.

"No," Picasso answered. "It took me all my life."

That's how I feel about the work I do. My skills—as a marketer and small-business builder—are very valuable. If you want me to help you sell your products or grow your business, you can expect to pay me at least $2,000 an hour.

And that's only if I have the time . . . the work time . . . left in my schedule. If you want me to work during my personal time—evenings or weekends or during my vacation—how much would it cost you? You don't want to ask.

A wealthy businessman who has been reading *Early to Rise* for years has been trying to persuade me to help him grow his business. Recently, he offered to pay me $50,000 to spend a weekend with him—plus "plenty more" if I agreed to provide ongoing support.

I graciously turned down his offer, and he had a hard time understanding why. "I'm offering to pay you $3,000 an hour," he said.

That's true. For 16 hours (two days' work), $50,000 amounts to just a bit more than $3,000 an hour. But I didn't want to do it, because he was asking me to give up my personal time—the time I spend with my family and friends and the time I spend on my hobbies. And that time is worth at least twice as much as my working time.

How to Calculate Your Hourly Worth

Now, let's talk about you. Let's talk about how to calculate what your time is worth.

Here's the formula I use: Take the amount of money you earn per year. Then divide that by 50 weeks and then by 40 hours.

For example, my friend Walt has a growing real estate business. To convince him that he shouldn't be doing so much of the grunt work himself, I helped him apply my formula to his situation.

Walt makes about $150,000 a year. $150,000 divided by 50 weeks equals $3,000 (his weekly income). $3,000 divided by 40 hours comes to $75.

"That's how much your work time is worth," I told him. "So never do anything yourself that you can have done for less than $75 an hour."

Now you do it. Divide your yearly income by 50 weeks. Then divide that by 40 hours.

If the number you come up with is less than $50, it tells me you are not practicing a financially valuable skill—one that contributes to your company's bottom line. That means being involved in product creation, marketing, sales, or profit management. If that's the case, get yourself into one of those jobs . . . because that's where the big salaries are.

At the same time, make yourself as valuable as you can be at your present job. And start focusing on the really important work that will propel your career—and your income—forward.

Before long, your hourly rate will be double or even triple what it is today.

And your personal time will always be worth even more.

It might be three times as valuable as the time you spend at work . . . five times as valuable . . . or ten times as valuable. Only you will know just how much it's worth to you. But at the very least, your personal time should be worth double what your work time is.

Once you know what that number is, you can make sure that every personal task you engage in is "worth" that amount of money to you.

Let's say, for example, that, by applying my formula, you have calculated your work time to be worth $25 per hour. And you figure your personal time is worth twice that: $50 per hour. Let's also say that you spend three hours every weekend in the summer doing yard work (mowing the lawn, trimming hedges, fertilizing, and so on). Ask yourself if you think it's worth $150 ($50 times 3 hours of your personal time). If you feel it is, keep doing it. If it's not, hire someone else to do it—which you can certainly do for a lot less than $150 a week—and free up your time for activities you really enjoy.

Same goes for any household job that you can hire out—cleaning, painting, washing the car.

We all have the same number of hours in the day. How much you get paid for the hours you work—and how much pleasure you get from the hours you don't—are both up to you.

WHAT IT REALLY TAKES TO BECOME WEALTHY

"I don't have your attitude," Jeff said to me. "I just don't have the mind-set of someone who can make a lot of money."

"Do you want to make a lot of money?" I asked him.

"That's the sad thing," he said, smiling wryly. "I do."

"Well then," I said, "why don't you forget about your attitude and focus on your behavior?"

"What do you mean?"

"Why don't you stop thinking about why you can't make a lot of money and do something to make it happen?"

"Such as?"

I handed him a piece of paper. "Start by writing down how much you'd like to be worth in 20 years."

He did it.

"Now," I said, "let's talk about how you can build up to that number, year by year."

By the end of an hour, he had net worth goals for 20 years running. His target for the current year was very achievable. He was motivated.

"This is great!" he said.

"How do you feel about it?"

"I think I can do it."

Attitude can change behavior, but it is much more common for behavior to change attitude.

To put it another way: Getting wealthy doesn't depend as much on whether you are a positive person or a negative one as it does on the specific actions you take, or fail to take.

There is so much misinformation about this subject in the self-help industry.

The wannabes out there want to believe there is a mental switch inside them that, if they could find it, would instantly transform them from couch potatoes to human money machines.

"The switch is somewhere in your brain," they argue. "Find it, trip it, and the rest is easy."

Yes, it is easy to become wealthy . . . but if the only thing you are willing to do is *think about getting richer*, you are going to be disappointed.

You may not like what I'm saying, but you need to hear it. Please trust me on that.

I am not saying that I don't believe in positive thinking. I absolutely believe that it helps in many ways.

When I brush my teeth every morning, I smile at myself in the mirror at least a dozen times to give me energy and put me in a productive mood. And when I'm going to give a speech, participate in a wrestling match, or make a presentation, I use visualization to mentally prepare myself to do well.

But those things are not going to turn me into a money magnet.

To develop the power to create wealth, you need to take certain very specific wealth-building actions. And each time you complete one of those actions, you will feel a deep change inside you.

That's what you really need—a change in your wealth-building habits and behaviors.

PAY YOURSELF FIRST AND GET RICH AUTOMATICALLY

Take any financial planning book in a bookstore and you'll see the same advice. If you want to accumulate enough money to retire someday, begin by budgeting.

By listing expenses and limiting spending, they argue, you can have enough left over every month to save and grow rich.

The problem is that when you budget, you pay everyone else first—the landlord, the credit card companies, the phone company, and so on. And, despite your best efforts, you end up with next to nothing to put in the bank.

So you chastise yourself and promise to do better next month. But you never do.

There are always unexpected bills to pay, unanticipated sales to take advantage of, and that impossible-to-figure-out $200 or $300 that seems to fall through the cracks.

I tried budgeting for about 20 years. It just didn't work. But there is a strategy I discovered later on that *does* work. In fact, it works very well.

And I think the reason it works so well is because it is so damn simple.

Here it is: Every time you get paid or make a profit or come into money from any source, put a fixed percentage of it into a savings account right away. Put that money away *before* you pay any of your bills.

Think of yourself as a corporation. As CEO of that corporation, your job is to make a healthy profit. The money you put into this special account is your profit. Everything you spend after that—on bills and so forth—is your expenses.

Only the portion that goes into the savings account is really yours.

You might say, "This is nothing but a way to fool myself. If I have discipline, I can put the same amount of money into that account after I've paid my bills." You might even think doing that is more responsible.

But it's not. Your first responsibility as an individual (and as CEO of YOU Incorporated) is to become financially independent. By doing so, you will never be dependent on other people or the government. You will be able to take care of your needs and the needs of your family. That is a very responsible goal. And it's one that you will be able to achieve easily if you pay yourself first!

To make the process somewhat automatic, have a portion of your paycheck electronically deposited into your account each month. You could argue that this is actually paying yourself *second*. The government always gets first dibs on your paycheck. But you can beat the withholding tax racket by setting up a tax-deferred retirement account—an IRA, SEP, 401(k), or 403(b).

I pay myself first by depositing a percentage of any income I receive into a savings account. Then I put as much money as I'm allowed into a tax-deferred vehicle.

I pay the government next by creating a separate holding account into which I deposit a percentage of every fee that's paid to me—the money I'm going to owe in taxes.

Then I pay my bills.

If you are not doing this now, try it. You'll be amazed at how fast your personal profit account grows.

THE BEST WAY TO RISE TO THE TOP OF ANY BUSINESS

What's the best way to surpass your peers and outdo your competitors?

Work harder than they do.

If that sounds daunting, consider this: Most people don't work very hard.

Some spend their workdays doing as little as they possibly can. Lots more stay busy but achieve very little. They write long memos, discuss issues that don't need much discussion, contest insignificant points, and attend to the tedium.

But only a very few apply themselves—long and hard—to the key challenges that determine success.

Understanding this, you can see that even a modest amount of hard work will put you beyond both the terminally slothful and the lump-along middle crowd. Just by working smart nine hours a day, you will eventually rise to the top echelon of almost any organization.

But getting up the last rung of that ladder will be tough.

At that level, you are competing against other hard and smart workers. And some of them may have advantages you lack. They may be brighter. They may be more personable. They may have better contacts.

But there is one thing they don't have more of than you do—and that is time.

If you can spend more time than they are willing to spend or use your time more effectively, you *will* move ahead of them.

Fact is, life isn't fair. When it comes to money, beauty, intelligence, and talent, the distribution is uneven and arbitrary. But one thing we are all given equally is 24 hours a day. What you do with those hours is what will determine your success and happiness.

FIVE SECRETS TO DOUBLING YOUR MONEY EVERY THREE YEARS

To double your money every three years, you need an average yearly profit of about 26 percent. Does 26 percent seem like an easy target? Or a hard one?

When I look at my own investing track record, here's what I see.

- **Stocks:** I buy mostly no-load index funds and some blue chips. On average, over the years, I've done about as well as the market has done over the past 100 years—that is, about 10 percent. I do believe I could do better with stocks. I know plenty of people who do. If I followed their advice consistently and carefully, I believe I could get 15 percent to 18 percent a year on my stocks. That's not enough to double my money every three years, but it could still make me rich over time.

- **Low-Cap Stocks:** I tried them for a while and lost lots of money. So I stopped.
- **Bonds:** I buy AAA munis and I don't trade them, so I get market rates. Over the past 25 years, I've probably averaged about 4.5 percent—which, at my tax bracket, amounts to about 7 percent before taxes. Seven percent doubles every nine years. That won't increase my wealth significantly, but it will protect it from stock market losses and (usually) from inflation. I have about 50 percent of my liquid investments—15 percent of my net worth—in bonds.
- **Options:** Never tried them.
- **Currency Trading:** Never did it.
- **Rental Real Estate:** I've been doing this for about 20 years. I've gotten better with experience. Counting my early mistakes, I've averaged about 18 percent. I am very happy with my rental real estate investments, and I think that by applying what I've learned I can do a little better in the future. I wouldn't expect to earn 26 percent a year in real estate, though.
- **Buy-Build-and-Flip Real Estate:** I got into and out of this game with good timing. I made millions during the 1990s—making 50 percent or 100 percent on individual transactions almost seemed "normal." As prices became insane, I pulled out. (All of this was documented in *Early to Rise*.) And except for the foolish mistake of letting a partner buy three houses that I knew with certainty were overpriced in 2002, I never lost money on a deal. Overall, I averaged about 30 percent to 35 percent per year, annualized over 10 years, but I don't believe I will have this opportunity again for a long time. I do like the idea of investing in other areas (which Justin Ford recommends), and I'm doing some of that. But I'm not expecting 26 percent on these investments.
- **Passive Real Estate Investing:** I've been investing in a friend's real estate deals for about 15 years. The returns have been up and down—and I've had a chance to learn a lot about the development business during that time—but overall my ROI with him has been about 14 percent.
- **Overseas Development:** I bought a lot of overseas real estate in the past 15 years. My returns have been generally very good

on that—50 percent or better. But I am not doing much of it now. It has become a much more selective market.

- **Small Businesses:** The one area of investing that has given me the greatest returns—well in excess of 26 percent—has been my investments in small businesses. Although individual businesses that I'm involved in vary greatly (a few lose money, a few linger at breakeven, a few make modest profits, and a handful hit the jackpot), I've probably averaged more than a 50 percent per-year return for the first 10 to 15 years on all of my start-up ventures. Counting the older businesses, too (which have much slower equity growth) and the occasional failures, I would say that my overall ROI on small-business investments has been more than 35 percent.

Start-up businesses have given me so much—a steady growth of income, a base of wealth that has doubled every three years, the opportunity to get involved in so many other, interesting investments, and a rich and stimulating business life.

Because of the nature of what I did—getting involved in dozens of start-up businesses, including two direct-marketing companies that were essentially holding companies for start-ups, I've had the chance to participate in hundreds of launched businesses over the past 25 years. I've seen, and made, every mistake that you can possibly imagine. And I've seen some very successful launches, too.

Although I sometimes grouse about working too hard, I have to admit that I love starting new businesses. It's so much fun. And it's something I know how to do. When I start a business these days, I am confident it will work. I didn't always have that confidence. And I didn't always deserve it. But gradually, over 25 years, I accumulated a little guidebook in my mind that gives me good advice on what will work and what will not.

In 2007 I transcribed that mental book onto paper. The result was my best-selling book *Ready, Fire, Aim*, published by John Wiley & Sons.

So if you were to ask me, "What is the absolute fastest way to become rich?" I'd have to answer: by starting a small business.

That's my answer. It doesn't mean it is your answer. You may not want to invest the time, creativity, and energy that it takes to be a successful entrepreneur. You may be retired already and determined not to give up your daily golf game. If investing in your own small business is not for you, then I recommend you look into stock investing and real estate. I don't think you should expect to safely double your money every three years that way, but you can certainly do as well as or better than I have.

But if you do think you'd like to be an entrepreneur, you will be rewarded for it. Not only can you double (or even triple) your money every three years, you can also enjoy the many other benefits of being your own boss:

- The freedom to choose your own schedule.
- The power to create your own products.
- The excitement of being fully challenged.
- The knowledge that you are providing an income for your employees.

My friend Anna W. asked me to help her start a business based on her love of music. She'd been looking over her current retirement plan and figured out that if she keeps her present job and continues to increase her responsibility and her income, she will be able to have a comfortable retirement in 14 years (at age 67).

That's not bad. Most people in her age bracket won't do that well.

But if she puts her energy and resources into creating a successful business of her own, she can look forward to a much better return on her "investment."

Anna is going to start her new business on the side, working evenings and weekends. She's going to find a partner to back her, develop her product, and take it to market. When we went over the numbers, it became clear to Anna that this secondary business—if it is successful (and I'm pretty sure it will be)—will allow her to achieve her retirement goals in 5 years instead of 14, while she is still relatively young.

At that point, she can do whatever she wants to do with the rest of her life.

That's what a business can do for you.

Think about your own financial situation. Are you okay as you are—or would it be helpful to triple your money every three years?

If you need that kind of way-above-average ROI in your life, you simply have to consider starting your own business. Don't quit your day job. Just get something going on the side. You don't have to invest a ton of money or work endless hours. You can do well starting small.

Here are five proven (and absolutely true, in my experience) secrets of highly successful entrepreneurs that will help turn you into a business-building genius.

Secret Number 1: Don't Spend Too Much Time Planning

When you are entering a market, you don't know (and couldn't possibly understand) the hidden problems and challenges you will face. You won't understand those problems until you make a few mistakes. And you won't solve them (and go on to making a success of your new business) unless you are capable of changing directions quickly.

Most successful new businesses (probably 90 percent of them) end up following practices that are different than anticipated. That's why it doesn't pay to spend too much time and money planning. Do a reasonable amount of noodling. Figure out the big strokes and give yourself a bail-out option. Then go for it. He who can adapt wins.

Secret Number 2: Don't Spend Too Much Money

The vast majority of business start-ups that succeed do so on a limited budget. Almost none of them have the benefit of venture-capital funding.

The great majority of new businesses are hampered (and enhanced) by flying on empty. People involved in businesses that have limited funds must think harder, work harder, and (most important) sell harder. Their primary initial effort is to bring in the cash. And that's how it should be. There is only one thing that will surely stop any business in its tracks—and that's a lack of money. Ironically, limited capital usually means a quicker and stronger cash flow.

Secret Number 3: Get Operational Fast

The most common reason for new product/project failures is wasting time getting ready. Between making overlong and expensive business plans, endlessly tinkering with the product, fooling around with focus groups, and second-guessing yourself, it's easy to let a good product/project lose its steam.

Bootstrappers don't mind starting with a copycat idea targeted to a small market. Imitation saves the cost of market research—and the start-up entering a small market is unlikely to face competition from large, established companies.

Secret Number 4: Go for the Quick Cash First

Contrary to what some business books tell you, successful entrepreneurs admit that they take the fastest route to cash when launching a new venture. They do so because they don't have a choice. (See Secret Number 2.) After the cash starts coming in, they have the time and funds to improve the product, enhance customer service, and refine operations.

Keep in mind that the best-laid plans are often arrogant. You don't know for sure how to best serve the market. When launching a new business or product, figure out how you can get to breakeven fastest. This kind of noodling will force you to pay closer attention to the market.

Secret Number 5: Forget About the Crack Team; You Are It

Successful entrepreneurs don't hire experts to run their businesses. They figure it out for themselves. When it comes to making your new product/project work, rely on nobody but yourself to make sure it gets done right. It may be stressful and time-consuming to do a lot of extra work, but it will pay in the long run. You will understand the project in an intimate, extremely valuable way.

HOW TO THINK LIKE A BILLIONAIRE

In his thoroughly entertaining book *The Prime Movers*, Edwin A. Locke gives this example of the way entrepreneurs think:

An average person observes evergreens growing along the roadside and thinks that they look pretty, especially when partly covered with snow. At this point, his thinking stops. An entrepreneur observes the same trees and thinks, "These trees would look good in people's living rooms at Christmas. I wonder what people would pay for them?"

And he would continue to ask such questions as:

- How hard is it to grow evergreens?
- What investment is required?
- How big should they be before being cut?
- How difficult would it be to cut and transport them?
- How much would it cost?
- How long would they keep before losing their needles?
- Where would they be sold?
- What would the competition be like?
- Could I make other, related products—e.g., wreaths?
- Can I make money in such a seasonal business?
- How much?
- How can I get started?

This kind of active, directed thinking is one of the things that separate entrepreneurs from the rest of humanity. In fact, the most successful entrepreneurs in history—all of them mega-billionaires by today's standards—seemed to have dynamic, pragmatic minds.

Locke gives plenty of examples, including these:

- **Thomas Edison:** He was a "virtual thinking machine. Almost until the day he died, his mind poured forth a torrent of ideas, and he might track as many as 60 experiments at a time in his laboratory."
- **Steve Jobs:** He bombarded people with his ideas—his investors, his board of directors, his customers, his subordinates, and his CEO John Scully.
- **Henry Ford:** "He threw himself into every detail, insisting on getting small things absolutely right. . . . But he never lost sight of the ultimate, overall objective. He had a vision of what his new car (the Model T) should look like. From all the improvisation, hard thought, and hard work came a machine that was at once the simplest and the most sophisticated automobile built to date anywhere in the world."

You may be thinking, "Hey, I'm no Thomas Edison or Steve Jobs or Henry Ford." Well, neither am I. And I could rattle off a dozen multimillionaire entrepreneurs I know who don't have that kind of brain capacity, either.

Raw intelligence is not the issue. If it were, Einstein would have been wealthy. What matters in the world of commerce is *how* you think.

Some people, whether because of their upbringing or their DNA, have a natural billionaire mind. But just about anyone who is smart and ambitious can learn to think like a billionaire.

You can transform your mind completely and permanently in a matter of a few short months by making small changes, one at a time. It will take some effort, though. As Joshua Reynolds once said, "There is no expedient to which a man will not resort to avoid the real labor of thinking."

Begin by vowing to talk to every successful person you know or meet. Tell them how much you admire what they have accomplished and ask them how they do what they do.

You may be amazed at how open they will be to such inquiries. Nine times out of 10, they'll be eager to tell you just about everything they know.

Unfortunately, many of the twentieth century's greatest entrepreneurs have been disparaged by historians and the media. As Locke points out in *The Prime Movers* (2000), if you mention the names Andrew Carnegie or John Rockefeller or Cornelius Vanderbilt to most people, they think "greedy robber barons who took advantage of their circumstances." They know nothing about their accomplishments. What they know, for the most part, is based on persistent myths that prevent them from learning from these men and prospering.

Locke says:

It is often claimed that the Prime Movers have been viewed with suspicion at best and with distaste or repugnance at worst. . . . The most basic motive [of those who envy them] is . . . hatred of the good for being good . . . It is hatred of the Prime Movers because they are intelligent, successful, and competent, because they are better at what they do than others are.

The ultimate goal of the haters of the good is not to bring others up to the level of the most able (which is impossible) but to bring down the able to the level of the less able—to obliterate their achievement, to destroy their reward, to make them unable to function above the level of mediocrity, to punish them, and, above all, to make them feel unearned guilt for their own virtues.

When you become super-successful, you'll have to learn how to handle the people who are going to resent you for achieving what they themselves have been unable to do. But first, you have to get yourself into that enviable position. And you do that by practicing the thinking of the great entrepreneurs who thought like billionaires and, so, amassed billions.

If you study someone with a billionaire mind-set—discover exactly how they do what they do by figuring out how they think—you may be able to "upgrade" your brain to one that will allow you to have the kind of life they enjoy.

To get started, here are some observations I've made from studying great wealth builders such as Jobs and Edison and Ford:

1. A "normal" person is concerned with protecting his ego. When dealing with a problem he doesn't really understand, he pretends he understands the contributing factors and doesn't try to find out what anyone else thinks. A person with a billionaire mind asks questions incessantly. He has no ego when it comes to learning. He knows that knowledge is power.

2. A "normal" person has a consumer mentality. He looks at a hot new product and thinks about how he would like to own one. A person with a billionaire mind has an entrepreneurial mentality. He looks at it and thinks, "How can I produce this or something similar in my own industry?"

3. A "normal" person is wish-focused. He daydreams about making gobs of money. A person with a billionaire mind is reality-based. He is always analyzing his own success and the success of others and wondering how he could learn from it.

4. A "normal" person, when confronted with a challenging idea, thinks of all the reasons why it might not work. A person with a billionaire mind sees the potential in it and disregards the problems until he has a clear vision of how it might succeed.

5. A "normal" person resists change. A person with a billionaire mind embraces it.

6. A "normal" person accepts the status quo. A person with a billionaire mind is always looking to make things—even good things—better.

7. A "normal" person reacts. A person with a billionaire mind is proactive.

8. A "normal" person looks at a successful business owner and thinks, "That guy's lucky." Or "That guy's a shyster." A person with a billionaire mind thinks, "What's his secret?" And, "How can I do that?"

Start by being humble and asking questions. Do this until it becomes a habit. Then take on another characteristic of the billionaire mind—like looking at a successful new product and thinking, "How can I do something like that?"

Go through the list, mastering one characteristic at a time, and within three months you will be able to create new businesses almost automatically. You will become a natural leader. Money will flow to you like water coming down a hill. And then you'll be ready to deal with all the "normal" people who are jealous of your incredible success.

HOW NATURAL-BORN BILLIONAIRES FEEL ABOUT CHANGE

In Part Seven, I said that the average person is resistant to change, whereas the person with a billionaire mind-set embraces it.

That was simplistic.

In fact, most people—intelligent or otherwise—are resistant to change. That's because the instinct to distrust change is encoded deep in our DNA.

But our reluctance to change is also a matter of logic. Change creates confusion, and confusion creates extra work, and extra work creates stress. And stress is both unpleasant and unhealthy.

So why did I say that the average mind resists change while the mind of the billionaire embraces it?

Let me tell you a story . . .

Ten or twelve years ago, when half of the bestselling nonfiction books were about the Internet, some of the smartest young executives in my largest client's company came to him with a plan. They wanted to "revolutionize" the business by taking it online and changing from a direct marketing–based model to an advertising-based model.

He listened carefully to their proposal. He was excited about the prospects that the new medium offered and was happy that his people were brimming with ideas. But as they detailed their plan, he got a gnawing feeling in the pit of his stomach.

"It's an interesting approach," he said when they finished their PowerPoint presentation. "But I don't really understand how that would be profitable."

There were eight profit center managers in the room. And most of them had worked with my client long enough to know that they couldn't take his words literally. They knew that what he meant was, "That sounds like the craziest idea I've heard in a long time."

But one of them did take him literally and went about setting up an online profit center based on an advertising model. He spent millions of dollars and more than three years on it.

Meanwhile, my client started an online newsletter. But it was based on the old model he knew, direct marketing—and guess what? It gradually became a $20 million business and is, today, a core part of a $50+ million online publishing franchise.

Now if I ended the story here, you might suppose that the point of it is that it is wise to resist change. Indeed, it is natural and wise to resist change, but it is dumb to refuse it. There is a big difference between resisting change and refusing it. And that difference is the difference between an average person and someone who thinks like a billionaire.

This will be clear when you hear the rest of the story . . .

In making the comment he did, my client discouraged seven of the profit center managers who were present from moving to an advertising-based model. But he did not try to dissuade the eighth one from pursuing the new idea. On the contrary, he encouraged him to try. He knew that if seven-eighths of his business stuck with what they knew, the company could sustain a loss if the new idea failed completely. Which it did.

In other words, he was hedging his bets. Seven parts resisting change. One part welcoming it. That's how a billionaire thinks.

Here's a follow-up story . . .

Several years later, my client had the opportunity to buy a financial magazine published in England that was struggling at the time. Magazines are advertising based. Normally, he wouldn't be interested. But with this one, he thought he could reinvent the modern magazine. So, against all odds, he bought the publication and reinvented it by creating an online feeder to it and using direct-marketing techniques to sell back-end products.

The result? Five years later, it is the most successful financial magazine in London.

Those two stories are a good illustration of what I'm trying to explain today: the difference between how change affects an average person and how it affects a natural-born billionaire.

It's not that the person with a billionaire mind-set is *not* resistant to change. It's that he is willing to embrace it when he sees the benefit in doing so.

But there's another thing.

The natural-born billionaire doesn't jump at every opportunity he sees. He doesn't automatically embrace change just because it *might* offer him a benefit. No. The natural-born billionaire is more practical than that. His chances of benefiting have to be good.

In my client's case, he was willing to take a chance on the idea of an advertising-based online business, but only if seven out of eight of his profit center managers were doing things the traditional way. Seven out of eight is about 85 percent. In other words, he was willing to risk only 15 percent of his resources on this new idea.

What are the payoffs for the person with a billionaire mind-set?

There are two: money and ego gratification.

This is an important point. Natural-born billionaires are not completely or even deeply motivated by money. The real payoff for them is the feeling of accomplishment they get when they do something new and prove to the world that they have what it takes to be successful.

Most successful people will not admit to that, but it's true.

So now, let's get back to what I said about the average person being resistant to change, while the person with a billionaire mind-set embraces it. And let's try to say something less simplistic and more useful about the way a natural-born billionaire thinks.

The average person resists change completely because all it represents to him is extra work and stress. But the natural-born billionaire sees through the stress and work to the potential reward at the end: a financial and emotional bonanza.

Examples of people and companies and industries that resisted change and lost are too numerous to mention. Detroit automakers are the most obvious example. But it has also been the story (and the fate) of book publishers and newspapers and magazines—with the notable exception of the *Wall Street Journal* and the *New York Times*, both of which made an intelligent, well-calculated move to the Internet when the opportunity presented itself.

That is the key to thinking like a billionaire. You have to know when to resist change and when to welcome it. For me, it's a matter of how far away you are willing to go from what you know.

The average person doesn't want to go any further than he is forced to go. The would-be entrepreneur is willing to go far afield—to try things he knows nothing about. But the natural-born billionaire goes only one step further than he can see. I call it the one-step-removed principle.

Here's what I say about it in my book *Ready, Fire, Aim*:

> When developing new products, you don't want to make the mistake of investing in something that is two or more steps away from what you know how to do.
>
> That's because your chances of success decrease geometrically with each step. Take one step, and you are fine. Two steps, and you are on thin ice. Three steps, and you are up to your neck in very cold water.
>
> There are simply too many things you don't know about it . . . too many inside secrets that are blocked from your view.
>
> It is possible, of course, to succeed with a product that is wildly different from one you're selling now. It's just highly unlikely. Successful entrepreneurs take calculated risks—i.e., they act only when their calculations suggest they have a good chance of winning.

To think like a billionaire, you have to trust your instinct against change—but you must also train yourself to see change as having the potential for financial and emotional gratification.

You have to be able to calculate the odds of achieving the goal and calculate the financial payoff. And you have to be able to imagine how good you'll feel when all the naysayers (and there are always more naysayers than supporters) have to eat humble pie.

THE KEY TO ENJOYING A GREAT RETIREMENT (AND A LIFETIME OF HAPPINESS)

Close your eyes for a moment and picture yourself enjoying your ideal retirement. Perhaps you're standing knee-deep in a Montana river, fishing for trout. Or strolling through the streets of Prague. Or reading Faulkner on the back porch, listening to the sounds of your grandchildren playing in the yard.

Chances are, your actual retirement will look quite different from the way you're imagining it. For one thing, the kids playing in your backyard are more likely to be your great-grandchildren—because you'll probably retire a lot later than you think. If, that is, you retire at all in the traditional sense of the word.

A Vanguard survey released this year found that more than 60 percent of Americans (ages 40 to 69) indicated that they'll include some form of work in their retirement. A study by the Brookings Institution, a Washington think tank, had similar findings. As reported by CBS News correspondent Nancy Cordes, "Nearly 80 percent [of the study's participants] say they'll work on a part-time basis well beyond [age 63]." And the massive University of Michigan Health and Retirement Study (which surveys 22,000+ Americans over 50 every two years) also found that most Americans would prefer a "gradual retirement"—scaling back on their hours rather than quitting cold turkey—if they had the choice.

In a different sort of world—the kind of world that used to exist—retirement didn't involve work. You were part of an extended family. When you got old and wanted to stop working, you could do so. Your children would be running the family business. You would be consulted from time to time when important decisions had to be made. Your wisdom would be appreciated. Your instincts revered. You would be surrounded by your loved ones, enjoying the fruits of your combined labor. Everything would be lovely.

In the world we live in today, that doesn't happen. For one thing, you need money to retire well. A lot of money. So some baby boomers are going to be "forced" to delay their retirement because they simply won't be able to afford to stop working.

But even if you reach retirement age with millions in the bank, I'm going to argue that there's a more important reason for you to banish those dreams of an idyllic life of leisure.

To understand what I'm about to say, you have to understand this: Happiness in life comes not from idleness but from working. Not working at a job you hate, but working at tasks you care about.

Given that, the secret to a great retirement is to figure out how to get paid for doing work you would gladly do for free—and to be able to do that work when and where you want to.

Maybe you want to be a writer. Maybe your secret passion is cooking gourmet food. Maybe you've always wanted to get back into astronomy or archaeology or gardening.

Somewhere in your past is a buried profession—something you've long ago given up on. What if you could reprise that dream?

I know a man whose dream was to be a professional pilot. After working 30 years in the wallpaper business, he took my advice and got himself a job flying part-time for a small airline. A few years later, he became a part owner. He's making more money now doing what he loves than he ever made selling wallpaper. And he only "works" 20 hours a week.

My dad gave up a promising career in show business to become a teacher. Fifty years later, he went back into the acting business and became a professional actor. He acted in all kinds of commercials and soap operas, had small speaking roles in some big movies, and did some big spots in off-Broadway plays. He did it for 10 years, made some money, and had a great time.

The Internet has opened up a world of possibilities for "retirees." I met a guy who trades cigarette lighters online. This happens to be something he always wanted to do and planned to do once he stopped working. But by taking advantage of eBay and other Internet auction sites, he is already making more than $30,000 a year doing it just on weekends. Trading cigarette lighters!

There are plenty of other examples. You can become an Internet copywriter, an Internet editor, an Internet travel agent, or an

Internet teacher. You can make money giving marriage or dating advice on the Internet, or even selling underwear. You can use the Internet to make a living from your interest in wild roses, say, or your up-until-now useless knowledge about nineteenth-century swords.

For the best retirement possible, give up on the idea of playing golf all day. Instead, enrich your life with pursuits that mean something to you . . . and make money at the same time.

You can start your retirement planning right now by asking yourself the three Big Questions:

1. "What would I really enjoy doing?"
2. "Who would be the best person to do it with?"
3. "Where would I most want to do it?"

You may not be able to find a partner or relocate right away, but you can definitely start mastering the skills you're going to need for your new line of "work."

BECOMING A BETTER PERSON

In order to live a richer, healthier, more enjoyable life, you are going to have to make a commitment to:

- Pay less attention to yourself and more attention to other people.
- Focus on opportunities, not problems.
- Listen first, talk later.
- Criticize only when your criticism is helpful.
- Never speak badly about anyone.
- Never complain about anything.
- Perform an act of kindness every day.

This will have a profound effect on your happiness. Nothing else you do will bring you peace of mind. Money won't. Success won't. Fame won't.

The secret to substantial and enduring happiness has nothing to do with putting yourself first, nurturing your inner child, or any of the many other forms of narcissism so popular among today's pop psychologists. As someone who has spent too much time in the vain (and I do mean vain) pursuit of self-gratification, I am here to tell you that happiness and fulfillment in life is usually about doing less for yourself and more for others.

This is not a revolutionary concept. It was, it seems to me, the essential message of Christ and Gandhi, to name just two.

I'm probably not saying anything you don't already know. And you may be much further along than I am in making selflessness a permanent part of your life. Still, as I'm sure you've discovered, putting others first is a commitment that seems to require constant attention. And that is precisely why I am asking you—as I am asking myself—to renew that commitment now.

When I think about the happy people I admire, they are invariably those who are always looking out for others. I'm not speaking of missionaries and professional humanitarians but of ordinary people who make it a habit to care about those around them.

They are the people who ask you how you are doing and pay attention to your answer. They visit you when you are ill and have kind words for you when you need them.

They are ordinary people with the same problems that other ordinary people have—yet, they don't ask you to pity them. When they see you limping because of an injured knee, they don't tell you about their aching back. They give you sympathy and recommend a helpful treatment. When everyone gets up from the holiday meal and rushes off to have an after-dinner drink or smoke, they linger with the host—helping out by clearing the dishes or wiping off the table.

They know the names of your children. They remember your birthday. They know how you take your coffee. And though they want you to be better and stronger and more successful than you are, they never give you the feeling that they are unsatisfied with what you are, in fact, right now.

I am fortunate enough to be married to one of these people. My elder sister is the epitome of this type. And I have friends and even colleagues who fit the bill. I am always astonished by their goodness and humbled by their strength.

They make me want to be, a little bit each year, a better man.

Becoming a Better Person Starts with
Trying to Make the People in Your
Immediate Family Happier

Your spouse and children, mother and father, aunts and uncles, and nieces and nephews were not brought into this world to solve your problems. That's your job. Resolve to spend less time complaining to them and more time listening to their complaints.

Smile when you see them. Give them the time and attention they need to share their dreams and ambitions with you. Give them the advice they want and shut up when they don't want any. Become the person they turn to when the chips are down. Learn to love their peccadilloes and encourage them to overcome their faults.

Above all, be loyal to them.

Be a reliable and steady resource for your business colleagues, too. Help them achieve their goals—not because you want their support but simply because you want them to succeed.

And do something for people you don't know—a stranger you come upon, a foster child, or a sick or poor person who can benefit from your help. Spend money. Spend time. Most of all, spend your love.

Make this outward focus a natural part of your daily life. Do it purposefully and deliberately until it becomes second nature to you.

This is not the kind of goal one can achieve in a single year. It will be on my list this year. Perhaps it will be on your list, too.

CONCLUSION

In high school I was a proud member of Alpha Omega Theta (AOT), one of a handful of high school fraternities that flourished in Brooklyn and on Long Island during the 1950s and 1960s.

Like college fraternities, we hazed pledges, swallowed goldfish, sang fraternity songs, and threw up at beer parties. We also sponsored Little League teams and got into fights individually after school or in groups at local meeting places like the Rockville Centre Recreation Center or Nathan's Famous Hot Dogs in Island Park.

AOT was distinct among high school fraternities then because it didn't discriminate: composed mostly of Irish and Italian kids, we welcomed Blacks, Hispanics, Jews, and even WASPs into our fold. These were groups that were not welcome to join our rival fraternity: Omega Gamma Delta.

Most of us were working class or poor, but we did have a few members who lived in the wealthy part of town. What bound us was our Weltanschauung: We believed in the idea of fraternity—sticking together to help us get through adolescence.

And mostly, we did.

After high school, there was the natural disintegration of the graduating class, but at least two dozen of us kept in close touch. Of those, three died in Vietnam, one hanged himself in our train station coming back from Nam, four died of drug overdoses, one was killed in a fight, one got a life sentence for murder, and several went to jail for various reasons. Most of the rest spent their best years working dead-end jobs, drinking for comfort, and settling for much less than we wanted to when we were young.

But a handful succeeded. Peter P. and Joey M. started their own small businesses and lived well off the income till they retired. John F. became vice president of the New York Stock Exchange. Henry G. became a very wealthy bond trader. Peter W. made loads of dough working for the Rider Corporation. Kevin K. retired at 50 after a successful career in computers, and Richie B. became a big shot with the Republican Party.

Carl B. earned a good living in the hardware business but then contracted HIV, and Alec dissipated half his life with booze and cocaine but then rescued himself at 40 and now has a family and a successful business—two things he never imagined he would ever live to have.

My turnaround began in college, matured in Africa with the Peace Corps, and then accelerated in the early 1980s when I decided to become rich.

As a group we were not, obviously, favored by fate. But half of us survived, and, of those, a few of us managed to live lives we now feel proud of.

I often wonder about how much of that success was luck or fate, and how much came from the decision to change.

I can only speak truly for myself, and I must say that my transformation had very little to do with luck. It was a conscious decision I made when I graduated high school, a resolution to change my ways and climb out of the hole I had dug myself into.

I had no money or special gifts or friends in high places. I had wasted my education. I made my money painting houses and stealing clothes. I was a very marginal member of society, and that fact was apparent to my parents and siblings and to me. I was embarrassed to be who I was. I wanted to change.

But I always believed that I would one day become rich. And I always hoped that I would one day earn my living by writing.

These feelings drove me to change. But the only thing I could change was the bad habits that had kept me at the bottom of the social ladder.

I abandoned my drinking and fighting and carousing, and I devoted myself obsessively to study. For eight years I worked full-time and attended school full-time. I graduated college magna cum laude, earned a master's degree at the University of Michigan, and completed my Ph.D. requirements at Catholic University in Washington, D.C.

And then I spent two years teaching English literature at the University of Chad in Africa. It was there that I became fluent in French, learned passing Arabic, studied philosophy, and became a writer.

Since then I have written almost every day of my life both for my amusement and to advance my career. Five years later I had published my first best-selling book and earned my first million dollars. And since then I have continued to write and teach writing and accumulate more wealth than I or my children will ever need.

My experience taught me several things:

- Privilege is no assurance of success.
- Anyone, no matter where he starts from, can change his life for the better.
- Your best friends will always be your oldest friends—the ones who were loyal to you when you had nothing.

Looking back at my misspent youth, it is clear to me that the main thing that kept me from having the life I secretly thought I deserved was my own inability to change my behavior.

Once I accepted that fact and the need to change, everything started moving forward for me. And when the change came, it came quickly and continuously. I had setbacks, to be sure, but they never stopped my forward momentum because I wouldn't let them. I was hell bent on becoming the most successful person to emerge from my high school class—and not just from my disenfranchised fraternity brothers, but from all the wealthy and privileged kids, too.

I think I did it.

And that is the reason I believe so strongly in the capacity for personal change. It doesn't matter how bad things are for you right now. It doesn't matter if you have a lousy job or no job at all. It doesn't matter if you are earning minimum wage or even unemployed. It doesn't matter if you are in debt and overwhelmed and depressed. You can turn your life around as quickly and easily as you want. It all begins the moment you let your old self go and allow your inner person to become the person you know you have a right to be.

The purpose of this book was to provide a master plan for personal change. I have done my best to create a structure that contains every important lesson that I learned in my 40-year journey from under-achiever to the person I am today.

I feel confident that if you take the advice in this book seriously and put it into practice, you will experience the transformation you are looking for.

I'd like you to take a few minutes now and imagine, as clearly as you can, what that new life will look and feel like.

Picture your new house, your new car, your new career, and, most importantly, your new sense of personal power and financial independence.

Enjoy the feeling you have right now of knowing that you have a master plan in place that will give you everything you have just pictured.

And be happy to know that you can start enjoying the feeling of success and accomplishment immediately. You know what it takes. And you know how to do it.

In the beginning of this book, you discovered two important truths about what it takes to make a major change in your life:

- There is no obstacle greater than inaction.
- By doing something active—even something minor—your life will begin to change immediately.

You know now that *big* changes require *big* plans. And you have already made those plans. By creating your personal master plan, you have given yourself a blueprint for change. You know now how to achieve all your most important goals. And you know how to start enjoying the benefits of your new life immediately.

To create your master plan, you began by taking a formal inventory of your core values. You imagined yourself at your own funeral and discovered how you want to be remembered in each of the primary dimensions of your life. You used this experiment to identify important things about yourself that you might not have been aware you have.

Your next step was to use the funeral exercise to create lifetime goals. You wrote down those lifetime goals and now realize how critical it was to write them down.

Then, by following the process recommended in Part Two, you broke those lifetime goals into smaller units: seven years, one year, one month, one week, and finally daily tasks. I shared with you the technique I use to sort priorities. You were given all my best tricks for getting all your most important tasks done every day.

I shared my life-changing first-thing-in-the-morning routine. This routine combines the best idea I ever discovered about personal productivity with a secret I realized in a flash late one night when I had a few drinks too many.

This routine is the main reason I was able to accomplish more than a dozen lifelong goals. And these were goals I had been putting off for decades!

You learned a great system for keeping track of your accomplishments and motivating yourself to accomplish more. (All of the tricks, techniques, and routines you read about in this book are unique. Although they contain ideas I got from some of the best time management and personal productivity experts on the planet, the program—the master plan—is original.)

It is exactly what I used to quadruple my personal productivity—and I was pretty darn productive before I developed it!

You also learned:

- Why you *must* write down your goals.
- How keeping a daily journal can keep you on track.
- The Four Rules for setting goals that will greatly increase your chances of success.
- Why you should never check your e-mail, your voice mail, or your in-box first thing in the morning.

You accomplished all that in Part Two. If you put the ideas in that part into action, I'm sure you feel that you got more from them than you ever got from any other single source.

But it was only the beginning!

In Part Three, you learned more secrets about my early morning routine and how to organize your hours for maximum productivity. What's more, I told you my system for being on top of everything.

And not just your own responsibilities, but also those of all your subordinates. (Before I learned this system, my employees were getting away with murder. Now I know they will execute every task I delegate to them. That has given me a great sense of relief and has made every business I deal with infinitely more productive.)

And then you learned some very cool tricks for giving yourself hours of extra time each day. You may be using them right now to enjoy yourself or to get more accomplished.

If all that wasn't enough, you learned a profound secret for turning yourself into a success machine, and last, but not least, how to organize the perfect office. (It makes a big difference!)

You also learned:

- Why rising early will make you happier, healthier, and more productive—and 12 steps to make even the most dedicated late sleeper into an early bird.
- How much time you should dedicate to preparing . . . and how much to taking action.
- Why you shouldn't spend much time thinking about success.
- Which details matter, and which can be ignored.

But we didn't stop there.

In Part Four we talked about what many people have told me is the most important element of the master plan program.

This was the section in which I shared with you all the things I've learned from the smartest people I know about how to make the daily living of your life immensely richer. You learned about the choices you have every moment of your life.

You were given a way to instantly identify what choices would make your personal experiences richer and more rewarding. You also were given a way to identify which choices wasted your time or made you "poorer."

By eliminating the wasteful and/or destructive habits in your life, you developed the power to create personal abundance instantly, regardless of what challenges the outside world was giving you.

Perhaps more important than anything else, you learned the Zen secret of intentionality without desire. You learned how to accomplish much more without caring about the outcome. This is a mental technique that you can use for the rest of your life to keep disappointment and despair out of your life completely.

You also learned:

- How to overcome the three obstacles to taking action.
- Why rewarding yourself along the way is essential to achieving any goal.
- Five strategies for living a simpler, fuller life.
- What "emergencies" you can safely ignore in your life.

In Part Five you learned why positive thinking doesn't work for 90 percent of the people who practice it (which is why 90 percent of the people who preach it are perennial losers). You then learned what you have to do to be one of the 10 percent of those who profit from it.

I shared with you the "junkie's secret" for making as much money as you need, even if you have no resources to make money.

You discovered how to use doubt to your advantage, how and when to take the big leap, and another trick for keeping track of your progress. Finally you learned the only scientifically proven way to defeat the fear of failure.

You also learned:

- Why you can't wait for things to be "right" before you get started.
- The secret of Accelerated Failure.
- The one thing you must do to become what you want to be.
- When it's okay to doubt yourself.

In Part Six I shared with you some very original ideas about finding and profiting from a mentor.

Most people have no idea how much help the right mentor can be. I told you how to identify the person you need and how to persuade him to get into your corner.

It was here, too, that you learned the most important secret of being a powerful and charismatic leader, and how to triple your reading comprehension (and collect ideas that will truly benefit you).

You also learned:

- What ballroom dancing can teach you about leadership.
- How asking one question can change everything in your business and life.

- That mastering one skill can double your personal power.
- The secret of the 4-Hour Workday.

In Part Seven we talked about all the most important challenges to success—the traps and obstacles that stop even the most ambitious and talented people from succeeding.

We talked about overcoming information overload, the tyranny of e-mail, the nuisance of unwanted interruptions, intrusive demands on your time, ruts you can fall into, and, finally, how to defeat sadness before it becomes debilitating depression.

You also learned:

- What to do when disaster strikes.
- How to avoid the productivity-crushing power of information overload.
- When to ignore positive thinking—and when to embrace it.
- The secret to regaining passion for your life and work.

And as a bonus I shared with you some of my best ideas on building wealth in Part Eight.

In this part we talked about what wealth really means, how much wealth you really need, how to make wealth-building easy and even automatic. I told you my tricks for quickly rising to the top of any business, how to double your net worth every three years, how to incorporate change into your personal life and into the lives of your employees, and, finally, how to immediately "retire" and enjoy a lifetime of abundance starting tomorrow.

That's what you were given in this book. And I'm hoping that's what you have taken from it.

It's all there. Every idea, strategy, and technique I shared with you has been proven repeatedly through my personal experience. I know it works, because it worked for me.

So, if you haven't accomplished all this at this point, all you have to do is go back to the section you "missed," reread it, and put it into immediate action.

This is a book, not a magic pill. It contains all the ingredients you need to transform your life, but it won't work unless you use it. Use it by putting these ideas into action immediately.

You don't need to have any experience or prior knowledge to benefit from any of them. All you need to do is put them into action.

They will work even if you don't believe in them now. Suspend your disbelief. Follow the directions. Take action. Very soon you will be a believer.

The moment you begin acting on your master plan, your life will begin to change for the better. When you begin to see the tangible results—and they will happen immediately—you will feel very happy you made the decision to change.

As things change for you and you begin enjoying all the benefits of your new life, give back a little by sharing this book with others. You can give the book to those you want to help, but it would be better for you and for them (and for me!) if you convince them to buy the book, so they will have some skin in the game.

Remember, the protocol for success is ready . . . fire . . . aim.

You've read the book, so you are definitely ready. It's time to fire. Right now. Don't lose another day procrastinating. There will be time enough in the future to refine your master plan by changing little things here and there. But the time to act is now. Seize it!

ABOUT THE
AUTHOR

Michael Masterson is not your typical businessman. An ex–Peace Corps volunteer, he never took a class in business, doesn't read the business press, and doesn't like to talk business. He spends his spare time writing poetry, collecting fine art, and practicing Brazilian jujitsu. His neighbors call him a bohemian. But he's also an entrepreneur. He started his first business when he was 11 years old, and in the nearly five decades that have elapsed since then, he has played an integral part in dozens of successful businesses in a variety of industries.

The last business Michael admits to having helped launch is **EarlytoRise.com**, an Internet-based company that provides advice and training in "health, wealth, and wisdom." Started initially as an informal weekly e-mail to a handful of his protégés, it quickly morphed into a $28 million enterprise.

The primary focus of his business life these days, however, is as consultant to Agora Inc., a $300 million, Baltimore-based publisher of information products with offices in England, France, Spain, Germany, South Africa, and Australia.

Notwithstanding clandestine luncheons that erupt into new multi-million-dollar ventures, Michael insists that he has been spending most of his time teaching and writing since he retired, for the second time, when he turned 53.

He writes poetry and fiction ("somewhat badly," he says), as well as books on business and wealth building (all of which have been *Wall Street Journal*, Amazon.com, or *New York Times* best-sellers). "I have a readership that appreciates the way I look at things," Michael says. "And that is gratifying."

His nonfiction books include *Ready, Fire, Aim: Zero to $100 Million in No Time Flat*; *Seven Years to Seven Figures: The Fast-Track Plan to Becoming a Millionaire*; *Automatic Wealth for Grads . . . and Anyone Else Just Starting Out*; *Automatic Wealth: The Six Steps to Financial Independence*; *Power and Persuasion: How to Command Success in Business and Your Personal Life*; *Confessions of a Self-Made Multimillionaire*; and *Changing the Channel* (with MaryEllen Tribby).

The Pledge is his twelfth book and seventh with John Wiley & Sons. He continues to write about starting and developing small businesses on a weekly basis in the EarlytoRise.com e-zine.

INDEX